The Modernist Party

Edited by Kate McLoughlin

D1351421

EDINBURGH
University Press

For John and Brenda Shipman

Edinburgh University Press Ltd
The Tun – Holyrood Road
12 (2f) Jackson's Entry
Edinburgh EH8 8PJ
www.euppublishing.com

First published in hardback by Edinburgh University Press 2013

Typeset in 10.5/13 pt Sabon
by Servis Filmsetting Ltd, Stockport, Cheshire, and
printed and bound in Great Britain by
CPI Group (UK) Ltd, Croydon CR0 4YY

A CIP record for this book is available from the British Library

ISBN 978 0 7486 4731 6 (hardback)
ISBN 978 1 4744 0141 8 (paperback)
ISBN 978 0 7486 4732 3 (webready PDF)
ISBN 978 0 7486 8130 3 (epub)

Grateful acknowledgement is made to the Wyndham Lewis Memorial Trust for permission
to reproduce material previously published elsewhere. Every effort has been made to trace
other copyright holders, but if any have been inadvertently overlooked, the publisher will be
pleased to make the necessary arrangements at the first opportunity.

The Menu

A Note of Thanks

The Modernist Party began as a pedagogical idea. In the first meeting of a course on twentieth-century literature, I experimented with introducing the class to modernism through a discussion of parties (I have yet to meet a student who hasn't been to one). After exploring how people might feel before, during and after attending a party, we moved on to discuss the parties in Joyce's 'The Dead', Woolf's *To The Lighthouse* and Mansfield's 'The Garden Party', investigating how these scenes work formally and thematically in the texts. The students had already each researched a modernist figure of their choice – a writer, artist, dancer, musician, philosopher – and I then asked them to role-play him or her at an imagined party taking place in the 1920s. (I played Ernest Hemingway and was asked why I'd written such a gloomy ending to *A Farewell to Arms*.) The students and I mingled, introduced ourselves and made small-talk (no refreshments were provided, alas, and costumes and accents were not required). At the end, we discussed what we'd learned about our modernist fellow guests and how the role-playing had felt. 'Awkward', 'fun', 'embarrassing', 'hard to keep up the pretence' were among the responses: useful things to have learned about modernist experiences.

I would like to thank the students at the University of Glasgow and Birkbeck, University of London, who have played along with the modernist party experiment so sportingly. For their practical and intellectual help in delivering this volume, I am very grateful to Jackie Jones and the team at Edinburgh University Press, Anna Hartnell and Nick Trefethen. Finally, I owe major thanks to the contributors, with whom it has been a pleasure and a privilege to work.

Kate McLoughlin
Le Petit Pey, Périgord, 2012

The Guest List

Margo Natalie Crawford is an Associate Professor of English Literature at Cornell University. She is the author of *Dilution Anxiety and the Black Phallus* (2008), a study of the body politics of lighter- and darker-skinned blackness, and the co-editor, with Lisa Gail Collins, of *New Thoughts on the Black Arts Movement* (2006).

David R. Ellison is Distinguished Professor in the Humanities at the University of Miami, Florida. His publications include *The Reading of Proust* (1984), *Understanding Albert Camus* (1990), *Of Words and the World: Referential Anxiety in Contemporary French Fiction* (1993), *Ethics and Aesthetics in European Modernist Literature: From the Sublime to the Uncanny* (2001) and *A Reader's Guide to Proust's* In Search of Lost Time (2010).

Alex Goody is Reader in Twentieth-Century Literature at Oxford Brookes University. She is the author of *Modernist Articulations: A Cultural Study of Djuna Barnes, Mina Loy and Gertrude Stein* (2007) and *Technology, Literature and Culture* (2011), and the co-editor of *American Modernism: Cultural Transactions* (2009).

Susan Jones is Fellow and Tutor in English Literature at St Hilda's College, University of Oxford. She has published widely on Joseph Conrad, including *Conrad and Women* (1999), and is editing Conrad's *Chance* for the Cambridge Edition of the Works of Joseph Conrad. She has also written articles on modernism and dance and her monograph *Literature, Modernism and Dance* is forthcoming from Oxford University Press.

Kate McLoughlin is Senior Lecturer in English Literature at Birkbeck, University of London. She is the author of *Authoring War: The Literary*

Representation of War from the Iliad *to* Iraq (2011) and *Martha Gellhorn: The War Writer in the Field and in the Text* (2007), editor of *The Cambridge Companion to War Writing* (2009) and co-editor of *Memory, Mourning, Landscape: Interdisciplinary Essays* (2010) and *Tove Jansson Rediscovered* (2007).

Margot Norris is Chancellor's Professor Emerita of English and Comparative Literature at the University of California, Irvine. Her publications include *Virgin and Veteran Readings of* Ulysses (2011), *Suspicious Readings of Joyce's* Dubliners (2003), *Writing War in the Twentieth Century* (2000), *Joyce's Web* (1992), *Beasts of the Modern Imagination: Darwin, Nietzsche, Kafka, Ernst and Lawrence* (1985) and *The Decentered Universe of* Finnegans Wake (1976).

Jean-Michel Rabaté is Vartan Gregorian Professor in the Humanities at the University of Pennsylvania and co-founder and curator of Slought Foundation. He is an editor of the *Journal of Modern Literature* and a fellow of the American Academy of Arts and Sciences. He has authored or edited more than thirty books on modernism, psychoanalysis, art and philosophy. Recent titles include *1913: The Cradle of Modernism* (2007), *The Ethic of the Lie* (2008) and *Etant donnés: 1) l'art, 2) le crime* (2010).

Bryony Randall is Lecturer in English Literature at the University of Glasgow. She is the author of *Modernism, Daily Time and Everyday Life* (2007), co-editor of *Virginia Woolf in Context* (2012) and is co-editing Woolf's short fiction for the Cambridge Edition of the Works of Virginia Woolf.

Morag Shiach is Professor of Cultural History and Vice-Principal for Humanities and Social Sciences at Queen Mary, University of London. Her most recent books are *Modernism, Labour and Selfhood in British Literature and Culture, 1890–1930* (2004) and, as editor, *The Cambridge Companion to the Modernist Novel* (2007).

Angela Smith is Emerita Professor of English Literature at the University of Stirling. She is the editor of Katherine Mansfield's *Selected Stories* for the Oxford World's Classics. Her other publications include *East African Writing in English* (1989), *Katherine Mansfield and Virginia Woolf: A Public of Two* (1999) and *Katherine Mansfield: A Literary Life* (2000).

Nathan Waddell is Advance Research Fellow at the University of Nottingham. He is the author of *Modernist Nowheres: Politics and Utopia in Early Modernist Writing, 1900–1920* (2012) and *Modern John Buchan: A Critical Introduction* (2009). He is co-editor of *Wyndham Lewis and the Cultures of Modernity* (2011).

Joanne Winning is Senior Lecturer at Birkbeck, University of London. Her publications include *The Pilgrimage of Dorothy Richardson* (2000) and the edited *Bryher: Two Novels* (2000).

Introduction: A Welcome from the Host

Kate McLoughlin

Immanuel Kant's dinner-party

In *Anthropology from a Pragmatic Point of View* (1798), Immanuel Kant describes how to throw the perfect dinner-party. The company must not number fewer than the graces or more than the muses: a number from three to nine is 'just enough to keep the conversation from slackening or the guests from dividing into separate small groups with those sitting next to them'.[1] The conversation should proceed through three stages: 'narration' (which concerns the news of the day), 'arguing' (the exchange of opinions, which 'stirs up the appetite for food and drink') and 'jesting' ('the mere play of wit').[2] Governing all three phases are further injunctions: 'to choose topics for conversation that interest everyone', 'not to allow deadly silences to set in', 'not to change the topic unnecessarily', 'not to let *dogmatism* arise' and, should a serious conflict occur, 'carefully to maintain discipline over oneself and one's affects'.[3] These matters observed, a dinner-party will combine both physical good ('good living') and moral good ('virtue'), the former derived from fine food and wine, the latter from sociability and enlightenment. But, Kant cautions, a balance must be maintained 'whereby the inclination to good living is limited by the law of virtue'.[4] Have fun, that is, but not *too* much fun.

This recipe for an enjoyable evening out in late eighteenth-century Prussia provides a party paradigm. Kant presents his ideal dinner-party as a forum of enlightenment, culture, taste and progress, a notion of public–private[5] social interaction that, in the twentieth and twenty-first centuries, has been associated, by Jürgen Habermas and others, with the emergence of modernity.[6] In this model, the party itself becomes an art-form: the host a virtuoso conductor or choreographer (Kant refers to himself as managing his dinner-party[7]), the guests players or dancers. But haunting this event of intellectually stimulating discourse and gustatory pleasure is another version of the party, hinted at by Kant in his advice to maintain control over the self and its affects. This is the party as an occasion of excess, sensuous gratification, decadence, debauchery, violence and, ultimately, death. But the edifying gathering and the bacchanal are not necessarily separate events. Rather, they both inhere in every party's potential.

If preceding ages produced their own archetypal feasts – the Roman *convivium*, the Victorian dinner-party[8] – the party of the modernist period (roughly the last years of the nineteenth century and the first few decades of the twentieth)[9] fragments, like so many other phenomena, into diversity. In life and in literature, parties of the period range from tea-parties to cocktail-parties, from lunch- and dinner-parties to extended house-parties, from breakfast-parties to parties held in venues such as nightclubs, restaurants and artists' studios, from at-homes to dinner-dances to soirées. No attempt is made in the present volume to impose a definition of 'party', though the collection's emphasis is on individual, if recurrent, occasions rather than on more generalised salon culture or bohemian lifestyle. In these varying modernist parties, the twin propensities to constructive enlightenment and destructive excess (now with debts to Nietzsche, Freud and others) assume special resonance. The modernist equivalent of the Kantian dinner-party is the party – in real life and in text – which provides inspiration, food for thought and a model for creativity. This version of the party is often a forum for testing the relationship of the individual to other people, exploring the nature of the self and critiquing the state. But the party of the modernist period is also the party overshadowed by the first global, industrialised war: the vehicle for nihilistic experiences of despair and self-effacement leading to the debauchery of the death drive. In both its hypostasised ideal and its feared alternative, therefore, Kant's dinner-party provides an entrée to the modernist party.

Plato's drinks-party

The mechanics and mores of Kant's ideal dinner-party derive from Plato's *Symposium* (c. 385–380 BCE). The symposium proper – a drinks-party – takes place after dinner and entertainment. Host and guests having sated their appetites, they take turns to speak: each must deliver an encomium to the god Love. There is some hiccupping from Aristophanes[10] but, in Kantian fashion, he manages to recover himself and the seven speeches proceed in lively and dialogic fashion, drawing on a variety of rhetorical styles and moving participants and reader to more nuanced understanding. The modernist descendant of the symposium is discernable, *mutatis mutandis*, in the description by Virginia Woolf of a party given by John Maynard Keynes and Lydia Lopokova in July 1924:

> It was great fun at the party, enchanting, lyrical, Shakespeare with not a coarse word; and chaste conversation everywhere; dancing; the Davidsons, three of them,[11] hung with chandeliers and stately as caryatids [. . .] in a ballet designed by Duncan [Grant]. Lydia danced; we had a little fine champagne.[12]

The Keynes' party offered both physical and moral good in Kant's terms, and the contribution of hosts and guests to both is implicit in Woolf's description. The successful symposium, it emerges, is the outcome of accomplished party-giving and party-going.

The art of party-giving, as noted, requires considerable aptitude for choreography and orchestration. In January 1903, Joseph Conrad invited Ford Madox Ford and his wife Elsie to a birthday-party for the Conrad children; the description of the prospective party is reminiscent of a meticulously planned and scripted masque:

> Engulphing stops
> in the
> Natural course of things.
> Then
> The Young Lady
> Arises from her armchair
> and proceeding up the table on *her* right pulls a cracker with every feaster on that side. The Young Cavalier performs the same rite on *his* right side.
> Feasters don caps out of crackers.
> A Bell rings cheerfully![13]

The didascalia underscores not only the theatrical quality of the party, with assigned roles and movements, but also the sense of occasion; the same technique – a scenic description in the present tense – is used by F. Scott Fitzgerald to evoke a party in 'The Broken Lute' section of *The Beautiful and Damned* (1922). Setting requires as much attention as words and actions: guest-lists and seating-plans, as well as table decorations and menus, showcase compositional flair. In *Bohemia in London* (1907), Arthur Ransome conjures up a party-setting resembling 'a mad room out of a fairy tale':

> The walls were dark green, and covered with brilliant coloured drawings, etchings and pastel sketches. A large round table stood near the window, spread with bottles of painting inks with differently tinted stoppers, china toys, paperweights of odd designs, ashtrays, cigarette boxes, and books; it was lit up by a silver lamp, and there was an urn in the middle of it, in

which incense was burning. A woolly monkey perched ridiculously on a pile of portfolios, and grinned at the cast of a woman's head, that stood smiling austerely on the top of a black cupboard, in a medley of Eastern pottery and Indian goods.[14]

This might be a stage-set. In it, already visually and olfactorily stimulated, the guests drink 'opal hush' (a foamy, amethystine concoction of claret and lemonade) while the hostess croons 'O the googoo bird is a giddy bird'.[15] In her memoir/cookbook, Alice B. Toklas describes further sumptuous *mises-en-scène*: the symposiarch is now dramatist, now sculptor, now installationist. At a *gouté* (a lavish afternoon tea-party) in Beon, the dining room, exquisitely set for twenty or more, is 'elaborately decorated with pink roses'. The *châtelaine* calls the *valet-de-chambre* to place the *pièce de résistance* in the centre of the table, but, in a stunning *coup de théâtre*, this turns out to have been eaten by Gertrude Stein's poodle and must be replaced with a mere cake.[16] *The Alice B. Toklas Cookbook* takes the art–food connection even further, offering recipes entitled 'Bass for Picasso' and 'Oeufs Francis Picabia'.[17]

That the art of party-giving is related to the deepest sense of the creative self –particularly the female creative self – is made clear in Woolf's *Mrs Dalloway* (1925) and *To The Lighthouse* (1927) (more is said on this in Bryony Randall's chapter). In the former, Clarissa, taking her rest on the day of her party, is initially unable to work out why she is feeling 'desperately unhappy'.[18] Eventually, she locates the 'unpleasant feeling' in comments made earlier by Peter Walsh and her husband: 'but what had he said? [. . .] Her parties! That was it! Her parties! Both of them criticised her very unfairly, laughed at her very unjustly, for her parties.'[19] Clarissa's hurt is that of the insulted artist, her art-form that of the living sculpture or installation, inspired by her sense of people's separateness and her wish to bring them together: 'anyhow, it was her gift. Nothing else had she of the slightest importance; could not think, write, even play the piano.'[20] In the latter work, the same sense of anguished protectiveness towards her artistic creation is evident in Mrs Ramsay's reaction when her dinner-party is in danger of foundering on a guest's awkwardness:

'Will you take me, Mr. Tansley?' said Lily, quickly, kindly, for, of course, if Mrs. Ramsay said to her, as in effect she did, 'I am drowning, my dear, in seas of fire. Unless you apply some balm to the anguish of this hour and say something nice to that young man there, life will run upon the rocks – indeed I hear the grating and the growling at this minute. My nerves are taut as fiddle strings. Another touch and they will snap.'[21]

The fear of party failure expresses a sense of anxiety, widespread in modernist literature, relating to the viability and sustainability of the artistic work itself: an endemic textual tension. In another party scene – the Duchemins' breakfast-party in Ford's *Some Do Not. . .* (1924) – the fault-line shatters as the hostess's boorish husband, explicitly associated with Petronius' Trimalchio, disrupts the proceedings with lewd utterances. A guest blames the hostess for the collapse of the composition: '"I think this party's very badly arranged."'[22]

Mrs Duchemin is rescued in her agony by another guest who exhibits considerably greater talents as a party-goer. Party-going, as has been suggested, is as much an art-form as party-giving. Appearance is the first consideration in preparing the performance. In Douglas Goldring's description, Mary Butts, 'with her red-gold hair, white skin and glittering "boot button eyes"', was 'a gorgeous apparition at a party'; indeed, '[i]f two or three people were sitting quietly at a café table and Mary turned up, the group immediately became a party'.[23] Lady (Duff) Twyden (the inspiration for Ernest Hemingway's Lady Brett Ashley in his 1926 novel of protracted, nihilistic partying, *Fiesta/The Sun Also Rises*), 'dark, slant-eyed, long-nosed and of slighter build', made 'a perfect foil' for Butts.[24] 'I can see them now,' writes Goldring, 'entering together a crowded room [. . .] and "taking the floor" as duchesses ought to, but seldom do.'[25] The double entrance is a show-stopper, but it also implies a certain nervousness about effecting a solo arrival. Making an entrance, in costume, to a party is a cause of anxiety for Mabel Waring, the protagonist of Woolf's short story 'The New Dress' (?1925) (the author herself confided to her diary, '[t]he going into rooms properly dressed is alarming').[26] Aiming 'to be like them, pluming herself in fact', Mabel, as she glimpses herself in a mirror in her new dress, feels only 'humiliation and agony and self-loathing', convinced that the 'odious, weak, vacillating character' revealed by the party is her true self.[27] Performance anxiety may not be a uniquely modernist feeling – who knows what caused Aristophanes' pre-speech hiccups in *Symposium*? – but it has particular resonance in modernist literature, with its new, post-Freudian interest in interior states. The stakes of the performance have never been higher. Now that the crowds are larger, there are more witnesses of potential discomfort and the chances are greater of having to socialise with strangers (Nick Carraway, for example, meets his host for the first time during Gatsby's great party). The networks of communication are more efficient, ensuring that gossip can travel faster; in the era of high capitalism, competition is fiercer than ever. My own chapter, outlined later in this Introduction, considers performance anxiety on the part of that most reluctant of modernist party-goers, T. S. Eliot's J. Alfred Prufrock.

The party as performance, as display, as *do*, becomes more than ever an 'exercise in public relations' in the modernist period, when that industry was invented.[28] To give or go to a party is to signify information about wealth, class and status, to participate in a complex nexus of manufacture, commodification and advertising. Parties are marriage markets[29] and networking opportunities (more on this later). In such intense and demanding situations, conflict, awkwardness and embarrassment – all feelings that modernist writers sought to convey – are ubiquitous. Such feelings lead quickly to a sense of alienation, which can also be induced by the sheer banality of party interaction. The speaker of Herbert Read's 'Garden Party' (1919) confesses:

> I have assumed a conscious sociability,
> Pressed unresponding hands,
> Sipped tea,
> And chattered aimlessly
> All afternoon,
> Achieving spontaneity
> Only
> When my eyes lit at the sight
> Of a scarlet spider
> Running over the bright
> Green mould of an apple-tree.[30]

The need to assume 'conscious sociability' exposes the imposed and enervating artificiality of party conversation and behaviour which the poem conveys through the effect of inconsequentiality created by the shortness of the first seven lines. In a typical Readian gesture, the aimlessness is thrown into relief by an eye-catching natural detail and at this point colour vivifies the poem and enjambment speeds it up, dramatising the speaker's aroused attention. There is only one thing worse than being invited to a party like this: *not* being invited to it. For Clarissa Dalloway, being excluded from a party is a personal catastrophe:

> [T]he shock of Lady Bruton asking Richard to lunch without her made the moment in which she had stood shiver, as a plant on the river-bed feels the shock of a passing oar and shivers: so she rocked: so she shivered.[31]

These examples confirm the party's status as a sign rich in semantic content. 'Reading' a party yields a barrage of information about social position, means, leisure-time and gender roles; this semantic proliferation explains attempts at (excessive) control on the part of the symposiarch, whether in real life or in text.

The party as a work-of-art leads to the idea of the work-of-art as a party. This notion informs the chapters by Bryony Randall, Morag Shiach and David R. Ellison (the party as formal device is also treated by Susan Jones). Randall's chapter, 'Virginia Woolf's Idea of a Party', proposes the party as a new model for understanding the intertextual functions of Woolf's oeuvre. As Randall observes, Woolf wrote obsessively about parties and an 'intimate relationship' obtains between parties (or at least her 'idea' of a party, if not her actual experience of them) and her creative output. Taking what Woolf in *The Years* (1937) termed 'inconsecutive conversations' as a paradigm of interaction, Randall argues that the non-hierarchical party space constructed in Woolf's works from *The Voyage Out* (1915) onwards reflects the non-hierarchical relationship between them. In Randall's formulation, Woolf as writer/hostess throws a party in which her texts/guests 'dance, in light-spirited steps'.

In her chapter, '"Pleasure too often repeated": Aldous Huxley's Modernity', Shiach focuses on three kinds of Huxleyan repetition: quotation, circulating sexual energies and social rituals. Huxley's 'accumulating drops of allusion and quotation' represent not only a literary style but also 'the characteristic universe' of his fictional parties, 'where meaning emerges from the cumulative drops of fragmented conversation and quotation rather than presenting itself as continuous or coherent'. Serial sexual encounters at parties, together with the taking of narcotics, figure 'paralysis and obsessive return', while the 'repetitions and rituals' of 'enforced sociability' occasion psychic damage. Linking these symptoms in *Crome Yellow* (1921), *Point Counter Point* (1928) and *Brave New World* (1932) to Huxley's vision of modernity, Shiach explores how Huxley's textual strategies mimic party behaviours.

In 'Proustian Peristalsis: Parties Before, During and After', Ellison offers a reading of Proust's *In Search of Lost Time* (1913–27) in which the movement of characters through the social hierarchy and their expulsion from it, as evidenced by their inclusion in or exclusion from parties, illuminate narratological method. Proustian narrative 'flow', Ellison argues, can aptly be characterised by the pressure exerted by a frame on the party scene it encloses. Demonstrating the phenomenon with reference to the dinner hosted by the Duc and Duchesse de Guermantes in *The Guermantes Way*, the soirée hosted by the Princesse de Guermantes in *Sodom and Gomorrah* and the matinée hosted by the Princesse in *Finding Time Again*, Ellison provides a model of reading that links parties to ideas of excess and waste, a model which recognises the peristaltic tension and ease evoked in the reader consuming Proust's narrative.

Reading texts as parties opens up fresh ways of characterising both writing and reading: textuality as sociality; writer and reader as host and guest; intra- and extra-textual relations as social discourses (small-talk, talking over, conversation, interruption, miscommunication, quarrelling); narrative as the party arc from invitation to thank-you note; intertextuality as hospitality; rhythm as anticipation, fatigue and second wind; absorption as intoxication; authorial self-effacement and intrusion as shyness and showing-off; reader response as *RSVP*; and so on. This volume is itself susceptible to such a characterisation and more on this will be said at the end of this Introduction. But in addition to modelling works of literature, parties – real-life parties, that is – produce them. This is the subject of Joanne Winning's chapter, '"Ezra through the open door": The Parties of Natalie Barney, Adrienne Monnier and Sylvia Beach as Lesbian Modernist Cultural Production'. Winning explores the extent to which the Friday afternoon/evening parties given by Barney at the Temple de l'Amitié in her *pavillon* in the rue Jacob and the readings and gatherings hosted by Beach in her bookshop Shakespeare and Company and Monnier in her bookshop La Maison des Amis des Livres can be considered fora of intellectual work and literary productivity, as well as of levity and socialising (a Kantian combination). Drawing on the theories of Pierre Bourdieu, Winning suggests that, where cultural producers are rendered dissident by factors such as their gender or sexuality, the production of party space/time is a potential conduit via which they can define, establish and disseminate intellectual and aesthetic authority and hence shape literary output.

For Alex Goody, however, considering Gertrude Stein in her chapter '"Indeed everybody did come": Parties, Publicity and Intimacy in Gertrude Stein's Plays', the conduciveness to creativity of the public/private space of the party is ambiguous when the creativity in question is that of the host. As Goody recounts, Stein's publishing success with *The Autobiography of Alice B. Toklas* (1933) precipitated 'a disturbing invasion of her inner sense of self' in which her private interiority was 'opened out to the external world's values and definitions'. But this tension between publicity and private autonomy had already emerged as Stein and Toklas admitted the expatriate avant-garde to their domestic space at their parties in rue de Fleurus. Both parties and book success exposed Stein's private life to a publicity that threatened the sense of linguistic singularity with which she was investing her writing. This threat is textually mapped out in the plays Stein wrote about parties at the beginning and end of her career: *What Happened. A Play in Five Acts* (1913) and *A Play Called Not And Now* (1936).

The enormous intervention made by Barney, Monnier, Beach and Stein and Toklas in facilitating and developing the creativity of modernist writers and artists underscores the importance of parties to modernist networking. Understanding the significance of such networking has led to exciting new directions in modernist studies in recent years. Modernist network studies have explored the little magazines[32] and printing presses,[33] the coteries and salons,[34] the bookstores and publishing houses,[35] the tea-shops and restaurants[36] – but not the parties,[37] though Suzanne Churchill and Adam McKible explicitly voice the need for 'a "great party" model [of modernism], one that duly recognizes the era's sense of urgency, mechanization, and conflict but also addresses modernism's spirit of creativity, conviviality, and playfulness'.[38] Rightly so, for parties were of huge significance in extending patronage, forging creative alliances (and *mésalliances*), sparking productive disagreements and enabling knowledge transfer. Some of the great modernist parties were dazzling one-off set-pieces. Among these were: the party thrown by Sydney and Violet Schiff at the Hôtel Majestic in Paris on 18 May 1922 for Joyce, Proust, Picasso and Stravinsky, with Diaghilev, fresh from Ballets Russes triumphs, as guest-of-honour and master-of-ceremonies;[39] the party thrown on 1 June 1926 by Edith Sitwell in honour of Gertrude Stein, also attended by Woolf, E. M. Forster, Siegfried Sassoon, Tom Driberg and Arnold Bennett; and the two dinners held on 15 and 17 July 1914 at Dieudonné's restaurant in London, the former to celebrate Vorticism ('a great success, every one talked a great deal,' commented Ezra Pound),[40] the latter Imagism.[41] The Imagist dinner given by Amy Lowell and attended by the Pounds, Richard Aldington and H. D., Allen Upward, John Cournos, Henri Gaudier-Brzeska and John Gould Fletcher seems to have had a nasty, bullying note, as Upward read out a parody of Lowell's poems and Pound declared the Imagist school at an end.[42] 'The silver on the table glittered, / And the red wine in the glasses / Seemed the blood I had wasted / In a foolish cause,' wrote Lowell later in 'The Dinner Party' (1916).[43] The creative energy deriving from the party is not necessarily founded upon harmoniousness and civility. The dark side of Kant's ideal is beginning to make its presence felt.

Modernist partying was not solely a matter of great set-pieces. A number of renowned hosts gave regular parties, and here the party starts to blur with the phenomenon of the salon and with more generalised bohemian behaviour. Regular gatherings were held by Ford and Violet Hunt at their Kensington home, South Lodge, until 1914; attendees included Wyndham Lewis, Jacob Epstein, May Sinclair, Phyllis Bottome, H. D. and Aldington, D. H. Lawrence and Jessie Chambers, and Rebecca West.[44] Lawrence, Bertrand Russell, Augustus John, Katherine Mansfield and John Middleton Murry, Eliot and the Woolfs were regular guests at Philip and Lady Ottoline Morrell's legendary house-parties at Garsington (the parties in Lawrence's *Women in Love*, based on those at Garsington, are explored in the chapter by Margot Norris).[45] W. B. Yeats held court on Mondays at 18 Woburn Buildings (Pound, Cournos and William Carlos Williams were among the courtiers)[46] and T. E. Hulme did so on Tuesdays at Mrs Dolly Kibblewhite's house in Frith Street (Rupert Brooke and the Georgian poets, Pound, Aldington, F. S. Flint, Cournos, Ford, Lewis and other luminaries attended).[47] Emerald Cunard entertained the Sitwell brothers, Pound and Lewis in Cavendish Square, while Eva Fowler and Olivia Shakespear organised house-parties, teas and readings in Kensington.[48] Then there was Bloomsbury: 'noetic enclave', 'brand' and lived example of G. E. Moore's philosophy, expressed in *Principia Ethica* (1903), of 'the importance of beautiful objects and personal relations'.[49] Then there was the partying at restaurants – Pound at Pagani's and then Belotti's,[50] almost everyone at the Eiffel Tower Restaurant in Percy Street[51] – and at artists' studios.[52] In Paris were the great salons already mentioned – and more – while in New York the young avant-garde headed for Greenwich Village and the salons of Mabel Dodge on Fifth Avenue, depicted in Carl Van Vechten's *Peter Whiffle* (1922) and Max Eastman's *Venture* (1927),[53] the Stettheimer sisters on West 58th Street, and Walter and Louise Arensberg on West 67th.[54]

Several points emerge from this dizzying array of social occasions. The first is that the party-host/party-guest relationship exemplifies *par excellence* Pierre Bourdieu's notion of the 'field of restricted production' in which is achieved 'the truly cultural recognition accorded by the peer group whose members are both privileged clients and competitors'.[55] Joanne Winning's chapter explores this further. The second is that the creative stimulation provided by modernist parties is international and interdisciplinary. The third is that parties overlap, acquire subparties and side-parties, become composite (David R. Ellison and Margo Natalie Crawford both discuss the idea of 'after-parties'): another suggestive model for literary texts. The fourth is that listing parties is in some way to *create* a party, to group together elements between which exist affinities and dissonances. The list or *congeries* reveals itself as another party-mimicking trope.

As this party of parties also reveals, networking foregrounds the thorny question, of high interest to modernist writers, of the relationship of the individual to the group. The *OED* offers definitions for 'party' which, in their mutual near-exclusiveness, emphasise the commonly experienced dialectic of inclusion and exclusion: 'an individual concerned in a proceeding' (II) and 'a company or a group of people' (III). Parties both bring people together and keep them apart: indeed, as

Christopher Ames observes, the 'classic gesture' of literary party scenes is of the individual stepping aside from the crowd for a moment.[56] The ontological consequences of the party and the identity politics of party-hosting and party-going are explored in the chapters by Susan Jones and Angela Smith and in my own chapter.

In '"The dinner was indeed quiet": Domestic Parties in the Work of Joseph Conrad', Jones offers a reading which relates the gender and post-colonial politics of parties in three texts written in Conrad's mid to late career – *Under Western Eyes* (1911), *Chance* (1913) and 'The Planter of Malata' (1914) – to the formal and thematic implications of their serial publication. In these works, tea-parties and dinner-parties explore the potentialities and limitations of women's roles, and their stereotypical representations, in early twentieth-century societies (revolutionary Russia, Suffragist Britain and colonial Australasia) and act as narrative devices ironising the context of the texts' first appearance as serialised romances. As Jones illustrates, in *Under Western Eyes* and *Chance* Conrad suggests that 'a woman's limited power might most successfully lie in the role of party convenor' but this image of the hostess is overlaid with 'considerable scepticism'. In 'The Planter of Malata', Conrad exploits the dinner-party as a means to 'aestheticise the very disintegration of individual and social identities that prefigures the collapse of the colonial project itself'.

For Smith in '"Looking at the party *with* you": Pivotal Moments in Katherine Mansfield's Party Stories', the numerous party-givers and party-goers in Mansfield's short stories seek to project an image of themselves which is always undermined by 'a moment of disruption when the picture is skewed'. At such moments, when Mansfield's scrutiny reveals an aspect of the secret self, a protagonist approaches an often ultimately elusive epiphany. Smith locates these pivotal instants in 'Frau Brechenmacher Attends a Wedding' (1911), 'Sun and Moon' (1920), 'Bliss' (1918), 'Her First Ball' (1921) and 'The Garden Party' (1922): a woman humiliated at a wedding; a child's anguish at the destruction of an ice-pudding; the discovery of adultery; a girl insulted at a dance; the announcement of a death. Each disturbing moment erodes the protagonist's faith in the self's substantiality.

My own chapter, 'Prufrock, Party-Goer: Tongue-Tied at Tea', investigates social performance in the context of Habermas's theories of communicative action. The putative tea-party in Eliot's 'The Love Song of J. Alfred Prufrock' (written 1910–11) is, in Habermasian terms, a less than ideal public sphere; Prufrock and his interlocutors lack the necessary 'communicative competence' with which to reach common understanding. Disclosing the affinities between Habermas's ideas and the philosophies of Josiah Royce and F. H. Bradley (studied by Eliot at Harvard), the chapter explores why Eliot chose to locate communicative failure in an occasion so apparently benign as a tea-party. The party becomes 'an alien ritual, possible formally to describe but not to enter into [. . .] unsusceptible both to external explanation and to internal communication'. Small wonder that Prufrock gets stage-fright.

The party as a negative experience resonates with Lionel Trilling's suggestion that modernity is characterised by the loss of the (Kantian) belief that pleasure is a good and its replacement by a cult of 'unpleasure'.[57] Catherine Belsey comments:

> Trilling aligned modernist pleasure with the death drive. Whether or not this is the best way of explaining it, he surely judges astutely when he observes that the motive here is an alternative form of 'gratification'. In other words, unpleasure paradoxically offers its own forms of enjoyment.[58]

As Plato's drinks-party ends in chaos ('[e]verything went out of control; all there was left to do was to drink a great deal, and even that was completely unsystematic'),[59] it is time to tip-toe away and prepare to gate-crash the other great forerunner of the modernist party – Trimalchio's dinner-party – and experience the pleasure of unpleasure.

Trimalchio's dinner-party

The *Cena Trimalchionis* in Petronius' novel *The Satyricon* (?63–5 CE), invoked in a number of works of modernist literature,[60] is, to borrow Kant's description of 'feasts and great banquets', 'tasteless'.[61] Hosted by the boorish former slave and now wealthy Trimalchio, it features over-eating, over-drinking, ill-informed boasting, casual cruelty, serious bullying, spiteful gossip, drunken insults, lewd singing, competitive story-telling, lechery, showing-off, dog-fighting and violence. (Readers are invited to consider whether they would rather attend this or Kant's select gathering.) The courses arrive as ingeniously fashioned assemblages: in the entrée dish stands a donkey of Corinthian bronze bearing a double pannier crammed with olives; the *pièce de résistance* is a 'massive boar', baskets of date-filled vine-leaves hanging from its teeth, surrounded by 'tiny piglets of pastry', its flank sliced open to release thrushes.[62] Sensuous excess is at its height. And unsurprisingly, in the midst of this extreme living, is death, in the guises of the 'skeleton of silver' brought into the party, the description of Chrysanthus' funeral, the mock death-sentence pronounced on the slave-boy and Trimalchio reading out his will.[63]

Modernist variations on Trimalchio's dinner-party occur in real life and in texts. Douglas Goldring remembers Mary Butts as a 'child of her period, gathering rosebuds, experimenting (I suspect cautiously) with the drugs in vogue, and throwing more or less continuous wild parties'.[64] As the partying intensifies, inhibitions are lost, tongues loosened. Woolf told Roger Fry, 'parties [. . .] have the effect of making one do what one would in no other circumstances do'[65] and confessed to Jacques Raverat, 'I go to parties [. . .] and there get rather random headed and *say too much*.'[66] Edgell Rickword's 'Strange Party' (1922), set on the 'lawn's most secret shade' as 'cascades of the moon descend / on shadowy dancers with false cheeks of gold', captures the phantasmagorical effect of excessive party stimulation:

> Discreetly mocking in the gloom
> those masqueraders bow and twirl,
> feigning to exorcise the doom
> that seals the fountains of your heart, queer girl.[67]

The comatose melancholy recalls Keatsian negative capability: the 'droop[ing]', 'overweighed' girl is en route to oblivion. In contrast to this crepuscular moribundity, but sharing its nihilism, is the high-octane sleaze of perhaps the wildest party of all modernist wild parties, Joseph Moncure March's epic *The Wild Party* (1928). The hosts are Queenie and Burrs:

> Queenie was a blonde, and her age stood still,
> And she danced twice a day in vaudeville.
> [. . .]
> And she liked her lovers violent, and vicious:
> Queenie was sexually ambitious.
> So:
> Now you know.
> A fascinating woman, as they go.
>
> She lived at present with a man named Burrs
> Whose act came on just after hers.
> A clown
> Of renown.[68]

After a routine bout of domestic violence, Queenie and Burrs throw a (bootlegged) alcohol-, drug- and adrenaline-fuelled party in which Queenie will have sex with her friend Kate's date Black, and Burrs with Kate. *The Wild Party* is a syncopated medley of optical illusions ('Enormous blurred hands kept stealing / Spider-like, across the ceiling'); sacrilegious behaviour ('The way they drank was unholy');

sexual ambiguity ('ambisextrous'); confusion ('streamers of smoke'); noise ('like great hosts at war / They shouted: they laughed: / They shrieked: they swore'); copulation ('the party began to reek of sex'); grotesque physicality ('White arms encircled swollen necks'); violence ('They jostled: / Stepped on each other's toes: / Elbowed: / Clawed'); and detritus ('Bleared glasses stood / Half-empty, bottles stuck to wood. / Cigarette stubs: / Ashes / [. . .] A pink stocking: a corkscrew / [. . .] And a wet towel, with a stained border: / All stirred together in wild disorder').[69] Ultimately lethal, the party ends in a chaotic tableau of bodies invoking sex and death:[70]

> The double bed was a tangled heap
> Of figures interlocked; asleep.
> Limp arms lay flung in all directions:
> Legs made fantastic intersections:
> White faces lay tossed back:
> Mouths gaped; hideous, black.
> Collars hung loose.
> White bosoms lay bared.[71]

And death will come again and again to the modernist party: to Mrs Dalloway's evening-party ('Oh! thought Clarissa, in the middle of my party, here's death, she thought'),[72] to Mansfield's 'The Garden Party', to 'The Broken Lute' party in *The Beautiful and Damned*, to the Misses Morkan's dinner-dance in Joyce's 'The Dead' (1914).[73]

The Trimalchian admixture of bodily excess and death offers itself almost irresistibly to a Bakhtinian reading. Bakhtin's carnival is a 'temporary liberation from [. . .] the established order', 'special condition [. . .] of the world's revival and renewal'.[74] The figure of this anti-authoritarian festivity is the eating, drinking, defecating, copulating, grotesque body. Bakhtin writes:

> The essence of the grotesque is precisely to present a contradictory and double-faced fullness of life. Negation and destruction [. . .] are included as an essential phase, inseparable from affirmation, from the birth of something new and better. The very material bodily lower stratum of the grotesque image (food, wine, the genital force, the organs of the body) bears a deeply positive character.[75]

In this vision, the party is a collective *carpe diem*; indeed, this eat-drink-and-be-merry outlook is owned several times in the *Cena Trimalchionis*.[76] The Bakhtinian carnivalesque underpins Ames's reading of parties in modern literature in *The Life of the Party* (1991), a work that informs this Introduction. For Ames (also drawing on Bede's account of life

vein, to examinations of the spaces mentioned by Blair, scholars have added explorations of metropolitan exteriors and domestic interiors, tea-shops, workplaces and the seaside.[94] Products of cognitive and social transformations of space into place ranging across the globe, as provincial as they are metropolitan, small examples of 'modernity at large',[95] chronotopes and heterotopes:[96] parties lend themselves naturally to analysis with the tools of cultural geography. And yet, in another sense, they defy them. Occurring in actual physical locations, parties have no inherent or lasting connection with their locales. Consequently, they foster an understanding of space/place that is peripatetic, event-driven and impermanent. Crucially, they also reintroduce the coordinate of time – brief and fleeting time – which further complicates the space/place axis with ephemerality and unrepeatability.[97] Studying the modernist party, then, is an opportunity – taken in this volume by Winning and Waddell – to rethink space, place and time, to engage with micro-modernisms (the single evening, the one-off lunch), to appreciate the potential of a phenomenon that is at once social and geographical experience and literary device.

It was promised earlier that a final word would be said about the party-like qualities of this volume as a whole. It is hoped that the chapters assembled here, like party-guests, talk to and differ from each other and the reader in productive ways, contributing different approaches and viewpoints. Not everyone could be invited (a limited guest-list meant that there was no room for Mary Butts, Mina Loy, F. Scott Fitzgerald, Henry Green or Evelyn Waugh, for instance), but those present constitute a diverse and international gathering, demonstrating that the party was at the centre of modernist writing and intellectual activity. If the intention is to host something closer to Kant's dinner-party than to Trimalchio's, this is not to underestimate the former's capacity for exhilaration and discovery.

Notes

1. Immanuel Kant, *Anthropology from a Pragmatic Point of View* [*Anthropologie in pragmatischer Hinsicht* (1798)], ed. and trans. Robert B. Louden (Cambridge: Cambridge University Press, 2006), p. 179.
2. Ibid., p. 181.
3. Ibid., pp. 181–2 (emphasis original).
4. Ibid., p. 178.
5. '[E]ven the largest dinner party is always only a private party, and only the state party as such is public in its idea,' explains Kant (ibid., p. 180).
6. See, further, my chapter in this volume.

7. Kant, *Anthropology*, p. 179.
8. Roy Strong, *Feast: A History of Grand Eating* (London: Pimlico, 2003), p. 7.
9. The application of the term 'modernist' to this period is fairly loose, and should be taken to include proto-modernist tendencies.
10. Plato, *Symposium*, trans. Robin Waterfield (Oxford: Oxford University Press, 1994), p. 20 §185d.
11. Angus and Douglas Davidson and George Rylands.
12. Virginia Woolf, *A Change of Perspective: The Letters of Virginia Woolf. Volume III: 1923–1928*, ed. Nigel Nicolson and Joanne Trautmann (London: Hogarth Press, 1977), p. 120.
13. Joseph Conrad, *The Collected Letters of Joseph Conrad. Volume III: 1903–1907*, ed. Frederick R. Karl and Laurence Davies (Cambridge: Cambridge University Press, 1988), p. 9.
14. Arthur Ransome, *Bohemia in London* (London: Chapman and Hall, 1907), p. 55.
15. Ibid., p. 58.
16. Alice B. Toklas, *The Alice B. Toklas Cookbook* (1954) (London: Serif, 1994), pp. 32–3.
17. Ibid., pp. 29–30.
18. Virginia Woolf, *Mrs Dalloway* (1925), ed. Morris Beja (Shakespeare's Head Edition) (Oxford: Blackwell, 1996), p. 90.
19. Ibid., pp. 90, 91.
20. Ibid., pp. 91–2.
21. Virginia Woolf, *To The Lighthouse* (1927), ed. Susan Dick (Shakespeare's Head Edition) (Oxford: Blackwell, 1992), p. 78.
22. Ford Madox Ford, *Some Do Not. . .* (1924), ed. Max Saunders (Manchester: Carcanet, 2010), p. 114.
23. Douglas Goldring, *South Lodge. Reminiscences of Violet Hunt, Ford Madox Ford and the* English Review *Circle* (London: Constable, 1943), p. 148.
24. Ibid., p. 148.
25. Ibid., p. 148.
26. Virginia Woolf, *The Diary of Virginia Woolf. Volume II: 1920–1924*, ed. Anne Olivier Bell and Andrew McNeillie (London: Hogarth Press, 1978), p. 239.
27. Virginia Woolf, *A Haunted House: The Complete Shorter Fiction*, ed. Susan Dick (London: Vintage, 2003), pp. 165, 168, 167, 166.
28. Strong, *Feast*, p. 293.
29. See Ford, *Some Do Not. . .*, p. 185: 'They [the marriages] were the product usually of the more informal type of dance, of inexperience and champagne.'
30. Herbert Read, *Eclogues: A Book of Poems* (London: Beaumont Press, 1919), p. 23.
31. Woolf, *Mrs Dalloway*, p. 24.
32. See Georgina Taylor, *H. D. and the Public Sphere of Modernist Women Writers* (Oxford: Oxford University Press, 2001); Sean Latham and Robert Scholes, 'The Rise of Periodical Studies', *PMLA* 121.2 (2006), pp. 517–31; Jason Harding, *The Criterion: Cultural Politics and Periodical Networks in*

Inter-War Britain (Oxford: Oxford University Press, 2002); Adam McKible, *The Space and Place of Modernism* (New York: Routledge, 2002); Faith Binckes, *Magazines, Modernism and the Avant-Garde* (Oxford: Oxford University Press, 2005); Suzanne Churchill, *The Little Magazine* Others *and the Renovation of Modern American Poetry* (Aldershot: Ashgate, 2006); Suzanne Churchill and Adam McKible (eds), *Little Magazines and Modernism: New Approaches* (Aldershot: Ashgate, 2007). Cited in Helen Southworth (ed.), *Leonard and Virginia Woolf, the Hogarth Press and the Networks of Modernism* (Edinburgh: Edinburgh University Press, 2010), p. 13.

33. See Southworth (ed.), *Leonard and Virginia Woolf.*
34. See Kevin Dettmar and Ian Watt (eds), *Marketing Modernism* (Ann Arbor: University of Michigan Press, 1996); Wayne Chapman and Janet M. Manson, *Women in the Milieu of Leonard and Virginia Woolf* (New York: Pace University Press, 1998); Mary Ann Caws and Sarah Bird, *Bloomsbury and France* (Oxford: Oxford University Press, 2000); Patricia Laurence, *Lily Briscoe's Chinese Eyes* (Columbia: University of South Carolina Press, 2003); Sara Blair, 'Local Modernity, Global Modernism: Bloomsbury and the Places of the Literary', *English Literary History* 71.3 (2004), pp. 813–38; Peter Brooker, *Bohemia in London: The Social Scene of Early Modernism* (Basingstoke: Palgrave Macmillan, 2007). Cited in Southworth (ed.), *Leonard and Virginia Woolf*, p. 2.
35. See Lawrence Rainey, *Institutions of Modernism* (New Haven: Yale University Press, 1998); John Xiros Cooper, *Modernism and the Culture of Market Society* (Cambridge: Cambridge University Press, 2004).
36. See Brooker, *Bohemia in London*; Scott McCracken, 'Voyages by Teashop: An Urban Geography of Modernism', in Peter Brooker and Andrew Thacker (eds), *Geographies of Modernism: Literatures, Cultures, Spaces* (London: Routledge, 2005), pp. 86–98.
37. Parties in the literature of the period and beyond it are the subject of Christopher Ames's *The Life of the Party: Festive Vision in Modern Fiction* (Athens: University of Georgia Press, 1991), but this work is not about modernist networking.
38. Suzanne Churchill and Adam McKible, 'Introduction', in Churchill and McKible (eds), *Little Magazines and Modernism*, pp. 1–18: p. 13.
39. See Richard Davenport-Hines, *A Night at the Majestic: Proust and the Great Modernist Dinner Party of 1922* (London: Faber, 2006), ch. 1.
40. Ezra Pound, *Gaudier-Brzeska. A Memoir* (1932) (New York: New Directions, 1970), p. 52; quoted in Brooker, *Bohemia in London*, p. 118.
41. See Brooker, *Bohemia in London*, pp. 114–23.
42. Ibid., p. 115.
43. Amy Lowell, *Men, Women and Ghosts* (New York: Macmillan, 1916), p. 338.
44. See Goldring, *South Lodge*; Violet Hunt, *I Have This To Say: The Story of My Flurried Years* (New York: Boni and Liveright, 1926); Brooker, *Bohemia in London*, pp. 56–7.
45. Brooker, *Bohemia in London*, p. 137.
46. Goldring, *South Lodge*, p. 48; Brooker, *Bohemia in London*, p. 59.
47. Brooker, *Bohemia in London*, p. 98.

48. Ibid., 105–6.
49. Cooper, *Modernism and the Culture of Market Society*, pp. 249, 245; the description of Moore's philosophy is from Peter Stansky, *On Or About December 1910: Early Bloomsbury and Its Intimate World* (Cambridge: Harvard University Press, 1996), p. 9, quoted by Cooper on p. 245.
50. Brooker, *Bohemia in London*, pp. 106, 113.
51. Goldring, *South Lodge*, p. 161.
52. Ransome, *Bohemia in London*, p. 70.
53. Daniel Aaron, *Writers on the Left* (New York: Oxford University Press, 1977), pp. 10, 12.
54. Cooper, *Modernism and the Culture of Market Society*, p. 244. See also Robert Morse Crunden, *American Salons: Encounters with European Modernism, 1885–1917* (Oxford: Oxford University Press, 1993).
55. Pierre Bourdieu, *The Field of Cultural Production: Essays on Art and Literature* (Oxford: Polity Press, 2004), p. 115.
56. Ames, *The Life of the Party*, p. 96.
57. Lionel Trilling, 'The Fate of Pleasure', in *Beyond Culture: Essays on Literature and Learning* (New York: Harcourt Brace, 1965), pp. 50–76; cited in Ames, *The Life of the Party*, p. 160.
58. Catherine Belsey, *A Future for Criticism* (Oxford: Wiley-Blackwell, 2011), p. 14.
59. Plato, *Symposium*, p. 71 §223b.
60. In addition to the quotation in *Some Do Not. . .*, already mentioned, the *Cena Trimalchionis* supplied the epigraph of Eliot's *The Waste Land* (1922) and the original title of *The Great Gatsby*, *Trimalchio in West Egg* – see P. G. Walsh, 'Introduction', in Petronius, *The Satyricon*, trans. P. G. Walsh (Oxford: Oxford University Press, 1997), pp. xiii–xliv: pp. xx, xxi, xli–xliii.
61. Kant, *Anthropology*, p. 179.
62. Petronius, *Satyricon*, pp. 23 §31; 26 §36; 30 §40.
63. Ibid., pp. 26 §26; 32 §42; 41 §52; 59 §71.
64. Goldring, *South Lodge*, p. 151.
65. Woolf, *The Question of Things Happening: The Letters of Virginia Woolf. Volume II: 1912–1922*, ed. Nigel Nicolson and Joanne Trautmann (London: Hogarth Press, 1976), p. 438.
66. Woolf, *Letters Volume III*, p. 78 (emphasis original).
67. Edgell Rickword, *Collected Poems*, ed. Charles Hobday (Manchester: Carcanet, 1991), p. 66.
68. Joseph Moncure March, *The Wild Party* (London: Martin Secker, 1928), pp. 9–10.
69. Ibid, pp. 27, 28, 30, 42, 51, 64, 64, 57–8, 89–90.
70. Ibid., p. 89.
71. Ibid., p. 91.
72. Woolf, *Mrs Dalloway*, p. 156.
73. See Ames, *The Life of the Party*, Pt 1.
74. Mikhail Bakhtin, *Rabelais and His World*, trans. Hélène Iswolsky (Bloomington: Indiana University Press, 1984), pp. 10, 7–8.
75. Bakhtin, *Rabelais*, p. 62.
76. Petronius, *Satyricon*, pp. 26 §34; 32 §43; 43 §55.

to the end of Empire in the psychological disintegration of the dominant figure of imperial romance.

This chapter follows recent shifts in Conrad criticism that have drawn attention to the reductiveness of the 'achievement and decline' thesis solidified in the 1950s with Thomas Moser's influential view.[3] Emerging from a New Critical tradition that invested in value judgements about what constituted a 'good' piece of art, the model of achievement and decline in Conrad's work tends to marginalise as inferior most of Conrad's fiction published after *Under Western Eyes*. The formal aspects of Conrad's earlier proto-modernist narrative strategies, with their destabilised narrative voices, temporal dislocations and explorations of subjective indeterminacy and dislocations of consciousness, were more conducive to assumptions about Conrad's contribution to modernism. The work of Conrad's later career, published after and including *Chance*, does not so easily fit the model of rigorous exploration of male identity. In his late phase, Conrad specifically courted the lucrative market for women readers of serial fiction and emphasised the romance plots and women characters of stories such as *Chance*, *The Arrow of Gold*, *The Rover* (1923) and *Suspense* (unfinished; published posthumously 1925); this late work fell into a category signalling, for some, a qualitative decline that coincided with an apparently cynical decision on Conrad's part to accommodate popular forms. Yet by the end of the twentieth century, the burgeoning of textual studies of modernism and analyses of periodical publication, serialisation and the popularisation of the fiction market in the early part of that century had opened up the field for rereading Conrad's late work in new critical contexts.[4]

With these critical models in mind, the later texts show the author's engagement in a freshly ironic dialogue with his contexts of publication. In these late works we can identify Conrad's appropriation of popular generic forms such as the romance, sensation fiction and melodrama, where Conrad frequently alludes to the visual lexicon of the paratextual material of the journals in which his texts are now appearing, and where illustration and advertising increasingly function as unsolicited and 'accidental' framing devices for the text. Far from losing interest in innovative narratorial modes, Conrad instead shifts focus. His greater emphasis on women in these stories owes much to his exploration of the way women are stereotypically presented not only in popular genres, but in a far wider sweep of European culture. He draws attention to the way the visual stereotyping of the serial market draws on classical and traditional images, producing a homogeneity and lack of ontological distinction in appearance and a widespread conformity to generic type. The publication of Conrad's texts in the serial market causes the author implicitly to identify the disjunction between the textual and paratextual/visual material of serialisation, generating a subversive tone in these late texts that contributes to the predominantly sceptical treatment of the *fabula* itself. Whereas the protagonist of *Lord Jim* dreams of being 'a hero in a book' (p. 6), Conrad's late fiction questions anew the 'market' for romance which now commodifies and popularises the heroic and the romantic in the distinctively materialistic contexts of modern magazine publication.

But Conrad does not limit his critique to the presentation of women. In a move that is consolidated by his own success in publishing in this context, Conrad frequently assimilated the devices of the popular romance into the formal strategies of the text – only to undercut the expectations of a 'popular' readership in his delivery of a sceptical closure that aligns itself more closely with literary modernism. Conrad addresses the formal and social implications of romance by dissecting the interaction of individual and society in the context of the social gatherings most common to this fictional form in the early twentieth century – to the parties associated with domestic interaction, namely the tea-party and the dinner-party.

I

Under Western Eyes and *Chance* follow each other in order of their publication, yet they belong to very different genres and have sometimes marked an artificial critical division of Conrad's work into 'major' and 'late' (or 'minor') phases of his career. *Under Western Eyes* is a political novel, a story of revolutionary activity, of loyalty, betrayal and double agency, whose chief protagonist seems in one sense to be an entire society – the nation of Russia – rather than an individual character. It was first published in instalments in the *English Review* and the *North American Review* from December 1910 to October 1911 – both sober and serious literary journals. In *Chance*, whose main protagonist is a woman, Conrad turns to a modern readership for serialised fiction (*Chance* was first published, with illustrations, in the 'women's pages' of the Sunday magazine of the *New York Herald* from January to June 1912) and enters into a new interrogation of the romance genre and its relationship to the presentation of gender roles. Both novels support a complex creative history, yet both belong to their contemporary political moment, and both intriguingly exploit a tea-party scene where we can trace continuities in Conrad's thematic treatment of the issue of feminism. Conrad's representation of the burgeoning area of contemporary feminist politics is far from straightforward, and while he promotes female autonomy in both novels, he is often sceptical of the potential for its achievement in existing social structures. Conrad produces an ironic, sceptical view of this movement, as he does of any political group or any rhetoric of political incitement. *Under Western Eyes* offers a parody of the 'revolutionary' figure in Peter Ivanovitch, who claims to support feminism yet treats women abominably, while in *Chance* Mrs Fyne, the feminist figure of the novel, advocates complete female liberation until it is her brother's marital relationship that is at stake, at which time she behaves as the most conservative of critics of the female in question. In their distinctive representations of feminism, we nevertheless find some striking continuities in their exploitation of the formal device of a tea-party as a locus of social harmony. The first ironises feminism in the context of Russian revolutionary politics. The second, if read in the light of Conrad's reassessment of the relationship between genre and gender as it is presented in the context of the serial market, produces a surprisingly new, modernist engagement with the feminist context.

It is typical of Conrad's grim sardonic humour that he uses the occasion of a tea-party – that most innocuous of social gatherings – to ironise the revolutionary activity of Ivanovitch, 'the great European feminist' character in *Under Western Eyes*.[5] Ivanovitch, an exiled Russian, operates at the centre of a group of political agitators in Geneva that is recruiting personnel to incite a prospective 'intrigue' in the Balkans, which, 'with some money [. . .] would set the Peninsula in a blaze and outrage the sentiment of the Russian people' (p. 219). The group's leaders include Ivanovitch, and the grotesque Madame de S—, a gothic caricature, or rather inversion, of Madame de Staël.[6] Madame de S—, we are told, 'was very far from resembling the gifted author of *Corinne*' (p. 142), but de Staël's *Lettres sur les ouvrages et le caractère de Jean-Jacques Rousseau* (1788) are elsewhere part of the context of the novel's themes (Razumov writes his 'confessional' journal under the statue of Rousseau in Geneva).

The revolutionaries are residing temporarily at the Château Borel, a run-down mansion outside Geneva, formerly belonging to a banker's widow. A bizarre tea-party takes place at this fading and disintegrated castle, which provides a gothic setting (Madame de S— is also described as 'a galvanized corpse out of some Hoffman's tale' (p. 215)) for the headquarters of Russian revolutionary sympathisers, who are planning insurrection from outside the national borders. The occasion encapsulates the coldly disturbing irony and hypocrisy surrounding the group's activities – at this point Ivanovitch and Madame de S— are

'sounding out' the credentials of a new recruit, a Russian 'exile', Kirylo
Sidorovitch Razumov, who has recently arrived from Russia. In an echo
of *Lord Jim*, Ivanovitch characterises Razumov as 'one of *us*' (p. 208,
emphasis original) – hoping he will be a good candidate for implement-
ing the latest plot, a 'man of energy and character, in view of a certain
project' (p. 210). The dramatic irony of the tea-party where Razumov
meets Madame de S— for the first time at the Château Borel does not
lie simply in the anti-democratic views of the so-called liberationists of
Russia (Ivanovitch declares that Russia's problems 'can never be bridged
by foreign liberalism' (p. 211)). It is exacerbated by our knowledge of
Razumov's activity as a double agent sent by the Russian government to
infiltrate the group.

In fact the tea-party carries with it many additional ironies, not least
in its ascription to Ivanovitch's character the epithet of 'the great feminist' (p. 212), while he terrorises the 'lady companion', Tekla, who acts
as his servant at the Château and follows him with unstinting devotion
in spite of his patronising and brutal behaviour towards her. While
she is trying to organise the tea-party, Razumov ascertains her fear of
'the burly feminist' (211). The scene is described with a note of black
humour:

> But with a preliminary sound of bumping outside some door behind him,
> the lady companion, in a thread-bare black skirt and frayed blouse, came
> in rapidly, walking on her heels, and carrying in both hands a big Russian
> samovar, obviously too heavy for her. Razumov made an instinctive move-
> ment to help which startled her so much that she nearly dropped her hissing
> burden. She managed, however, to land it on the table, and looked so fright-
> ened that Razumov hastened to sit down. (p. 217)

Neither does Tekla find female solidarity in the presiding figure of
Madame de S—, who is busy barking orders at Ivanovitch from her
reclining position: 'The rasping voice asked from the sofa abruptly –
"*Les gâteaux?* Have you remembered to bring the cakes?"' (p. 217).
As Madame de S— 'talked in a hoarse tone of the political situation
in the Balkans', Ivanovitch fetched the parcel of cakes, 'which he must
have extracted from the interior of his hat' (p. 217) and 'with imper-
turbable gravity he undid the string and smoothed the paper open on
a part of the table within reach of Madame de S—'s hand', while she
'extended a claw-like hand, glittering with costly rings [. . .] took up [a
cake] and devoured it, displaying her big false teeth ghoulishly' (p. 217).
Meanwhile, 'the lady companion poured out the tea, then retired into a
distant corner out of everybody's sight' (p. 217). The fake gentility of the
'revolutionary' gathering underscores the descriptions of Ivanovitch's

oleaginous attention to his hostess's needs (the suggestion that she may bankroll the plot prompts his behaviour).

Madame de S——'s wolfish gluttony and Tekla's attempts at servile invisibility add to the ironic presentation of the veneer of social politeness. Nothing more sharply defines the crumbling scenario into which the double agent Razumov appears in Geneva than the tea-party at the Château Borel, conducted in the manner of the de Staël salons, where the civilised niceties of sharing gâteaux, sipping tea and engaging in cultured conversation barely conceal the murky undercurrents of insurrectionary politics, the autocratic subtext of Ivanovitch's so-called feminism and the double agency lying at the heart of the novel.

Following *Under Western Eyes*, a series of deferrals caused delay to Conrad's completion of *Chance*, yet the creation of this novel overlaps in many ways with the production of *Under Western Eyes*, and we can identify some of the thematic continuities between the two novels when Conrad again uses the scene of a tea-party to critique a form of 'fake' feminism. In this novel, aimed at the women readers of the *New York Herald*, he turns back to the use of his dramatised narrator, Marlow,[7] framing Marlow's comments on women in the context of a more sceptical discussion of the 'woman question'.[8] But he also achieves a tighter ironisation of romance by bringing into play his responses to a new form of serial fiction in which he now aimed to present his work.[9]

The following discussion refers to a section from Chapter 2 of the book version of *Chance*. The dramatised narrator, Marlow, a retired seaman, tells his interlocutor about his visits to the country home of a middle-class couple, Mr and Mrs Fyne, whom he has befriended while taking a vacation in the English home counties.[10] It is through these visits that Marlow meets Mrs Fyne's friend, the young abandoned heroine, Flora de Barral. On the surface, the Fynes' is a highly conventional marriage, but Mrs Fyne is a feminist, writing a tract on women's education. Marlow is often invited to join the Fynes at an afternoon tea-party: 'I played chess with Fyne in the late afternoon, and sometimes came over to the cottage early enough to have tea with the whole family at a big round table'.[11] Like the strange tea-party at the Château Borel, the Fyne family gathering is hardly conventional and Conrad's narrator strikes a wry note, identifying a disjunctive tone to the social ritual:

They sat about [the table], a smiling, sunburnt company of very few words indeed [. . .] Mrs Fyne smiled mechanically (she had splendid teeth)[12] while distributing bread and butter. A something which was not coldness, nor yet indifference, but a sort of peculiar self-possession gave her the appearance [. . .] of an excellent governess; as if Fyne were a widower and the children

not her own but only entrusted to her calm, efficient, unemotional care.
(p. 37)

But others are present, in whom Mrs Fyne seems to show greater interest
than in her own children:

> The atmosphere of that holiday cottage was – if I may put it so – brightly
> dull. Healthy faces, fair complexions, clear eyes, and never a frank smile in
> the whole lot, unless perhaps from a girl-friend.
>   The girl-friend problem exercised me greatly. How and where The Fynes
> got all these pretty creatures to come and stay with them I can't imagine. I
> had at first the wild suspicion that they were obtained to amuse Fyne. But I
> soon discovered that he could hardly tell one from the other, though obvi-
> ously their presence met with his solemn approval. These girls in fact came
> for Mrs Fyne. They treated her with admiring deference. She answered to
> some need of theirs. They sat at her feet. They were like disciples. It was very
> curious. Of Fyne they took but scanty notice. As to myself I was made to feel
> that I did not exist.
>   After tea we would sit down to chess and then Fyne's everlasting gravity
> became faintly tinged by an attenuated gleam of something inward which
> resembled sly satisfaction. (pp. 37–8)

This episode sets the scene of Marlow's visits to the Fynes. However, it is
only in a later typescript with holograph emendations that Conrad adds
the remarks about Mrs Fyne's political and sexual persuasion that constitute the second paragraph of the above quotation. In the manuscript
that corresponds to the serial text, we hear nothing of Mrs Fyne's role
as proselytising feminist, nor do we hear of the pointed lesbian subtext
at this juncture in the narrative.[13] Only after the serialisation of *Chance*,
when Conrad was preparing his text for publication in book form, did
he add the paragraph beginning 'The girl-friend problem exercised me
greatly'.[14]

This passage shows how Conrad emended his narrative strategy in
two specific areas, both of which extend the role of feminist critique in
the novel. The first applies to narratorial positioning. His additions con-
tribute to the greater sense in the book version of Marlow's possessive-
ness over the story. In Marlow's somewhat dry and teasing tone there
is nevertheless a hint of his increasing paranoia (developed elsewhere in
the final book version), an anxiety about being marginalised from his
own story – 'As to myself I was made to feel that I did not exist.' He
also cuts Fyne's role, which in an earlier version suggested Fyne's attraction to the chief 'girl-friend', Flora. The book version shows Marlow's
textual and sexual appropriation of Flora unchallenged (he expresses
an erotic attraction to her victimisation), so that Flora's later rejection
of Marlow's chivalrous attitude to her and his misunderstanding of her

actions are more acutely refined. *Chance* is also the last time Conrad uses his dramatised narrator, Marlow – we hear a hint of his sense of redundancy in this line.

Conrad also draws on his familiarity with the social and political context of the narrative, particularly through allusion to a variety of popular contemporary texts. The 'girl-friends' resemble those popular or sensational, as well as controversial, fictional contexts like the New Woman novel, exemplified by Sarah Grand's *The Heavenly Twins* (1893), and something of the characteristics of Hardy's Sue Bridehead appear here in the combined presentations of Mrs Fyne and Flora. Conrad fleshed out Mrs Fyne's role as an ardent feminist, interested in the careers of her 'girl-friends', advocating female autonomy and writing books on women's education, although she apparently sustains a highly conventional marriage herself.

This passage not only gestures to the political context. Consider the line 'But I soon discovered that he could hardly tell one from the other' (p. 37). Marlow hints at the homogeneity of all those ubiquitous images of women to be found in contemporary serial publications. The moment initiates an overall shaping of the critique of female representation throughout the book, where the text constantly refers us to the limited nature of existing representations of women (including Marlow's). At this point it is important to remember that *Chance* was not Conrad's first encounter with a popular market.[15] As far back as 1901 'Amy Foster' had appeared in the *Illustrated London News*, in which an illustration for the first instalment shows the heroine in a 'picture hat', seated at the table with the family in a conventional conversation piece depicting tea-time in the iconography of Victorian genre painting. The caption for the illustration reads: 'She would help her mother to give tea to the younger children.'[16]

Conrad ironises Mrs Fyne's conventional image as hostess of a tea-party in his added paragraph to the book version of *Chance* by drawing attention to her powers of authority over the girls – 'She answered to some need of theirs' – and she replaces, in Marlow's view, the authoritative role of the husband or indeed himself as narrator. His presentation of Mrs Fyne's 'biblical' authority, with her disciples at her feet, manipulates the conventional role of hostess into a reversal of the customarily patriarchal role. As she takes leadership of what looks like a Victorian reading group, Mrs Fyne is given the role of a Mrs Pankhurst rather than of a Carlylean figure. But more importantly, Marlow's authority as narrator is also undermined – he is later challenged by his unnamed interlocutor, so that his presentation of feminism in the novel is shown up to be unreliable and driven principally by anxiety for his own role as convenor of the narrative.

Conrad has shifted the critique of Peter Ivanovitch's so-called Russian 'feminism' to the context of Suffragist politics in England, but essentially he does so by transposing the same ironic textual marker – a caricatured tea-party – from the debased 'salon' culture of European revolutionary gatherings to an English pastoral setting. In *Chance*, as Conrad revised his critique of romance in the light of the contexts of serial publication, he allowed for a wry perspective on the conventional marriage plot, where women preside over genteel conversation at tea-parties, and brought to bear on the text references forms of fiction associated with a female readership – the romance and the New Woman novel – and contemporary political references. But he also produced an astute reading of the representation of women in popular journals, with their highly visual component. He shows up the limitations upon women of the homogenising effect of syndication, of a dissemination of repetitious images to a wider public than ever before. Even the critique of patriarchy itself is open to the media's conventionalising effects. Marlow is himself quick to point out that Mrs Fyne corresponds to the popular visual image of the New Woman. In the chapter discussed above he describes her dress, in white shirt, jacket, tie and culottes, in a way that matches, in fact, an illustration for a *New York Herald* magazine feature of 1912 on the 'Joys of Women Walking'.[17] The representation of the feminist solidifies into yet another popular convention, rather as Conrad repeats the trope of the woman as hostess of salon parties in *Under Western Eyes*, 'The Warrior's Soul' and the *Arrow of Gold*, to suggest that a woman's limited power might most successfully lie in the role of party convenor, only to overlay the delivery of the image with some considerable scepticism.

II

Conrad sustained his critique of the popular market for fiction in his short story 'The Planter of Malata', which he finished in December 1913, soon after the completion of revisions to the serialised version of *Chance*. Here he also returned to the generic field of his first novels – *Almayer's Folly* (1895) and *An Outcast of the Islands* (1896) – which had both been associated by critics such as H. G. Wells with the context of imperial romance.[18] The 'Planter' of the story's title, Geoffrey Renouard, lives and works in isolation on his now successful plantation, where he produces silk on a small island (Malata): 'I see no one consciously. I take the plantation boys for granted.'[19] But he has just arrived in Sydney to gather 'information' (of an unspecified nature) from the editor and only as much as the mind acts, that is, expects, attends, remembers'.[25] The emphasis falls on mental activity and, as Ricoeur puts it, Augustine uses the example of reciting a poem from memory in order to mark 'the point at which the theory of distention is joined to that of the threefold present: Augustine's *distentio animi* (extension of the mind) offers a "solution" to the *aporia* of the measurement of time'.[26] Ricoeur's most effective move is to view Augustine's theory in the light of Aristotle's silence about the relationship between temporal experience and poetic activity in the *Poetics*. However, drawing attention to the emphasis on *activity* in both accounts, and on the creative, the making new by the effort of the mind, he shows the potential for reading Augustine's *distentio* in relation to the discordance or *aporia* inherent in narrative itself.

In relation to Ricoeur's account, Conrad's symbolic configurations of a physical event – in this case, the dinner-party in 'Planter' – within the narrative movement unify, in an Aristotelian sense, the beginning, middle and end of the tale of 'The Planter of Malata', but they also suggest the discordance 'inherent in narrative itself' by building on the reader's ironic association of each event (experienced each time anew by an effort of mental activity) both proleptically and analeptically. We read the event of the second dinner-party – the editor's account – in relation to Renouard's first attendance at the Dunsters'. We read the third party (a quiet dinner that turns into melodrama) in relation to the last two. And the final dinner on Malata in relation to all three previous events. The dinner-parties offer descriptive pauses, markers or discrete interludes that punctuate the narrative, but they also provide a chimeric overlaying, or Deleuzian repetition,[27] symbolically synthesising Renouard's journey of disillusionment and disintegration of identity. This structuring of the tale effectively metaphorises the mental activity suggested by Augustine's *distentio*, which allows us to experience temporal reality by a movement of the mind forwards and backwards in the threefold present. Conrad's presentation of the dinner-parties illustrates metaphorically and ironically the 'discordant concordance' that Ricoeur associates with the activity of the mind in relation to the experience of time and its recreation in poetic or narrative activity.

The reader's experience relies on her or his memory of the account of past events, attentiveness of the present and expectation of the future. But it also relies on a sense of imagined embodiment of these events (as in drama), in which the significance of each subsequent event, in this case a dinner-party, creates a dramatic irony that works on the reader to build a spatial pattern in the text requiring a highly sceptical reading. All subsequent dinner-parties described in the tale extend back in the reader's mind towards Renouard's recounting of his first meeting with

Felicia Moorsom at the Dunster dinner-party and his anticipation of future romance. Thus the Planter's absence at the final dinner, where he should be playing the role of host, anticipates the final dénouement, where Renouard joins the 'ghost' of the assistant in his own death. The assistant himself (and Conrad's initial working title for this story was 'The Assistant') symbolises an 'unhomely' repetition of a haunting absence throughout the text – a representation of the very *aporia* inherent in narrative identified by Ricoeur.

Conrad's use of parties in the texts of his later fiction suggests that we could do well to incorporate a reading of his responses to the context of serialisation in analysing his work of this period. At the same time, his use of the party as an aesthetic marker of these late texts offers a way of recovering this work from the assumptions of an apparent decline following *Under Western Eyes*, and, in the light of formalist perspectives, embracing a distinctive kind of innovation in the later fiction. In Conrad's words, his 'primary intention' in 'The Planter of Malata' 'was mainly aesthetic'.[28] In the context of this chapter, this argument needs to be placed in a wider setting of Conrad's relationship to the serial publication of his late work and in relation to two types of criticism of modernism – one largely historicist, focusing on contextual pressures as constitutive of the production of the work itself, and the other, developed in the light of current 'New Formalist' perspectives on modernism, that revises our assumptions about privileging historicist and contextual readings and encourages us to reassess the aesthetic structures of the work as work. On the one hand, exploration of the historical context of serial publication of Conrad's work has shifted the emphasis on more traditional forms of analysis of Conrad's oeuvre. On the other, a recent focus on formalist criticism in modernist studies enables us to recover the aesthetic focus of the later works as a distinctive aspect of Conrad's experimentalism that need not necessarily be eclipsed by his earlier, better known narratorial innovations.

Marjorie Levinson's 2007 article 'What Is New Formalism?' helpfully outlines the variations in approaches to radical transformations of literary study that recover the importance of form within (new) historicist perspectives.[29] While modernist attention to New Formalist criticism often focuses on the reading of poetry, a critic such as Richard Strier nevertheless offers a way into thinking about Conrad's late aesthetic practices by borrowing in large part from the theories of Peter Brooks, Erich Auerbach and Willard Van Orman Quine to emphasise how 'formal features of a text, matters of style, can be indices to large intellectual and cultural matters'.[30] Levinson believes that the strength of Strier's argument for keeping in play the 'value' of the literary work as an object of study arises because 'as a unit of analysis, a posit of significant form, [literature] so powerfully stages the tension between [. . .] two formalisms, the naïve and sentimental, the organic and artifactual, the necessary and contingent. It gives us unique access to the dynamic historical formation that inhabits the still form of form itself.'[31] Paradoxically, both historicist and formalist approaches to criticism converge to illuminate the 'modernist' features of Conrad's parties in his ostensibly revisionist later work.

Notes

1. Paradoxically, Conrad himself was renowned for his meticulous hospitality. Born in 1857 into the Polish landed gentry, he inherited the traditions of a host's responsibilities through family custom and through his Polish literary forebears – Adam Mickiewicz's national epic, *Pan Tadeusz* (1834), for example, is full of seigneurial feasting. In fact, Conrad sometimes transposes these inherited traditions into his fiction, such as the occasion of the feast in the compound at the end of section II of 'Karain: A Memory': 'That obscure adventurer feasted like a king' (*Tales of Unrest* [1898] (London: Dent Collected Edition, 1947), p. 17); or the captain's breakfast on board ship in 'A Smile of Fortune', where the host displayed 'a veritable feast of shore provisions' (*'Twixt Land and Sea* (1912) (London: Dent Collected Edition, 1947), p. 8). My thanks to Laurence Davies for identifying the more convivial gatherings of Conrad's work.
2. Joseph Conrad, *Lord Jim* (1900) (Oxford: Oxford University Press, 1983), p. 43. Hereafter page numbers are given in the text.
3. Thomas C. Moser, *Joseph Conrad: Achievement and Decline* (Cambridge: Harvard University Press, 1957).
4. See, for example, Ian Willison, Warwick Gould and Warren Chernaik (eds), *Modernist Writers and the Marketplace* (London: Macmillan, 1996); Lawrence Rainey, *Institutions of Modernism: Literary Elites and Public Culture* (New Haven: Yale University Press, 1998).
5. Joseph Conrad, *Under Western Eyes* (1911) (Oxford: Oxford University Press, 1983), p. 205. Hereafter page numbers are given in the text.
6. Anne Louise Germaine de Staël-Holstein (1766–1817), known as Madame de Staël, was a Swiss (French-speaking) author who mainly lived in Paris.
7. Marlow is a dramatised narrator in both 'Youth' and *Heart of Darkness*, written in 1898 and 1899 respectively and published in *Blackwood's Magazine*, but appearing together in book form in 1902; and *Lord Jim*.
8. For example, the militant phase of the Suffragist struggles in London had begun on 'Black Friday' on 18 November 1910. For an account of Suffragist history of this period, see Ray Strachey, *The Cause* (1928) (London: Virago, 1977).
9. See Susan Jones, 'Modernism and the Marketplace: The Case of Conrad's "Chance"', *College Literature* 34.3 (2007), pp. 101–19.
10. See Stephen Donovan, *Joseph Conrad and Popular Culture* (London:

Palgrave, 2005) for a discussion (in Chapter 2, on tourism) of the 'holiday atmosphere' as an organising principle of *Chance*, the intertextual resonances with popular contemporary texts on pedestrianism and the way in which the landscape as gendered space structures the novel.

11. Joseph Conrad, *Chance* (1913) (London: Hogarth Press, 1984), p. 37. Hereafter page numbers are given in the text.

12. Conrad has transformed the ghoulish 'false teeth' of Madame de S— into Mrs Fyne's dazzling natural set.

13. Joseph Conrad, MS *Chance* (holograph), Berg Collection, New York Public Library. In this manuscript, the second paragraph cited above has not yet been written.

14. Joseph Conrad, *Chance*, typescript with holograph corrections, Harry Ransome Center, University of Texas at Austin. In this document the second paragraph cited above appears for the first time, in Conrad's handwriting. I have identified this typescript as the text where Conrad made his most radical holograph changes to the serial version (between May and June 1913) before publication in book form (see Jones, 'Modernism and the Marketplace', pp. 108–12).

15. Conrad experimented with serialisation in popular periodicals from a much earlier moment than is sometimes recognised, although his success with *Chance* in the *New York Herald* Sunday magazine consolidated this trend. 'Amy Foster' appeared in *Illustrated London News* in 1901; essays that contributed to *The Mirror of the Sea: Memories and Impressions* (1906) appeared initially in *Pall Mall Magazine*, *Harper's Weekly* and the *Daily Mail* over 1904–6; all the stories from *A Set of Six* (1908) appeared variously in *Pall Mall Magazine*, *Harper's*, the *Daily Chronicle* and *Cassell's* between 1906 and 1908.

16. Gunning King, illustration for Joseph Conrad, 'Amy Foster', in *Illustrated London News* (14 December 1901), p. 915.

17. See Fanny Douglas's fashion column, 'Evolution in Dress: The Jacket', *National Observer* (1 October 1892), pp. 502–3, for an amusing explanation of the 'conventionalised' costume of the New Woman: 'It was as a riding-garment – as it were by strategy and under false pretences – that Woman won the Jacket for her own. She took Man's Vest and Hat at the same time, but deferred the annexation of his Breeches' (p. 502).

18. H. G. Wells, Review, *Saturday Review* (18 May 1896), pp. 509–10.

19. Joseph Conrad, 'The Planter of Malata', in Alexandre Fachard (ed.), *Within the Tides*, introduction by Laurence Davies and notes by Andrew Purssell and Alexandre Fachard (Cambridge: Cambridge University Press, 2012), pp. 13–73: p. 14. Hereafter page numbers are given in the text. For the sources and background to the tale see Davies's Introduction (pp. lvi–lvii), including a discussion of the geographical sources for the fictional 'Malata' (pp. lii–liii).

20. Frederic Dorr Steele's illustration of Miss Moorsom and Renouard shows the couple seated stiffly on the terrace, with the caption, 'She looked as though she were a being made of ivory and precious metals changed into living tissue', *Metropolitan Magazine* (June 1914), p. 27. Classical allusions abound throughout the visual lexicon of the tale. Felicia Moorsom displays the sculptured 'head of a statue', whose 'marble hair was done

and his dislike of them may well be reflected in 'Prufrock'. But there still seems to be a discrepancy between the perceived threat and the emotional response: is trivial party chit-chat really so repugnant?

Prufrock's fear is very specific. He is afraid that he will not be able to say a certain something in a certain situation. His sense of impending aphasia is formulated as a series of interweaved rhetorical questions: 'Do I dare?' (ll. 38, 45, 122); 'So how should I presume?' (ll. 54, 61, 68); 'how should I begin [. . .] ?' (ll. 59, 69); 'Shall I say [. . .] ?' (l. 70); 'Should I [. . .] / Have the strength [. . .]?' (ll. 79–80); 'would it have been worth it [. . .]?' (ll. 87, 90, 99, 100, 106). Numerous in their recurrences, the questions notoriously fail to identify the subject-matter of the intended utterance, reinforcing its absence and leaving it open to critical speculation ('not a lover's question but a metaphysical one,' suggests Lyndall Gordon, for example[13]). But the problem is not Prufrock's inarticulacy *per se*. Leaving aside for a moment the question of whether the poem represents its protagonist speaking aloud (and, if so, to whom), it is clear that he is capable of framing and phrasing his thoughts. His imminent aphasia is fluently, and therefore ironically, conveyed.

To what extent can Habermasian theories illuminate his difficulties? For Habermas, 'reaching understanding inhabits human speech as its telos'.[14] Habermas's philosophy, from *The Structural Transformation of the Public Sphere* (*Strukturwandel der Öffentlichkeit*) (1962) to *Europe: The Faltering Project* (*Ach, Europa*) (2008), has stressed the role of reason in coordinating action through human speech exchanges. In his earlier work, Habermas focuses on characterising the 'public sphere' in which exemplary speech exchanges took place; his later approach is a more trans-historical attempt to identify the qualities of speech exchanges by which action has been coordinated.[15] Throughout, his emphasis is on *rational* and *productive* communication, and the conditions which must obtain for it to be possible. Before applying his criteria to 'Prufrock', it is worth looking in a little more detail first at the ideal Habermasian venue for communicative action and then at the ideal speech situation.

Habermas characterises the public sphere in the following terms:

> The bourgeois public sphere may be conceived above all as the sphere of private people come together as a public; they soon claimed the public sphere regulated from above against the public authorities themselves, to engage them in a debate over the general rules governing relations in the basically privatized but publicly relevant sphere of commodity exchange and social labor.[16]

Such conditions first emerged in the coffee-houses and salons of the seventeenth century (Habermas cites the Glorious Revolution as the turning-point in Britain):[17] social venues in which a public made up of private citizens (albeit exclusively male) could engage in rationally based discussion and critique the state. Crucially, what rendered such venues 'ideal speech situations' was the fact that all those participating had an equal chance of having their say. Habermas continues:

> All speech exists in a context of actions and intentions. The mutual recognition of the subjects who communicate with one another includes the certainty that they can conduct themselves reciprocally towards one another's expectations, i.e. act according to valid norms.[18]

Further to this, participants in an ideal speech situation must possess 'communicative competence':

> [I]n order to participate in normal discourse the speaker must have at his disposal, in addition to his linguistic competence, basic qualifications of speech and symbolic interaction (role-behaviour), which we may call *communicative* competence. Thus communicative competence means the mastery of an ideal speech situation.[19]

A person with communicative competence is able not only to follow the linguistic rules for utterances in social situations, but also to empathise with an interlocutor's position. Specifically, a person with communicative competence is able to understand and judge 'validity claims', drawing upon a common fund of meanings and understanding that Habermas calls the 'lifeworld'. According to Habermas:

> The goal of coming to an understanding is to bring about an agreement that terminates in the intersubjective mutuality of reciprocal understanding, shared knowledge, mutual trust, and accord with one another. Agreement is based on recognition of the corresponding validity-claims of comprehensibility, truth, truthfulness, and rightness.[20]

For present purposes (as will be explained below), the most important of these is the third kind of validity claim: that to 'truthfulness'. In Habermas's terms, a 'speaker must want to express his intentions truthfully so that the hearer can believe the utterance of the speaker [can trust him]'.[21] In making a subjective truth claim – a claim to authenticity and sincerity – a speaker assumes obligations 'to prove trustworthy'.[22] These conditions in place, 'understanding' between the participants in a speech situation emerges.[23] In some contexts, this understanding is the foundation for coordinating action; in others, such as social conversation, it is the basis of non-purposive 'communication'.[24]

In assessing the communicative potential in 'Prufrock' against these

Habermasian criteria, it is important to note that the putative tea-party is not the only speech situation that obtains in the poem. Preparing the way for the party is a series of communicative instances in which Prufrock might potentially be engaged. In all of them, however, his participation is precluded. The voices he has known are obliterated 'Beneath the music from a farther room', and are 'dying' anyway (l. 53). The mermaids mentioned in the final lines sing exclusively 'each to each' (l. 124). The final line of the poem adverts, indeed, to the potentially lethal effects of intersubjective communication: 'Till human voices wake us, and we drown' (l. 131). Discourses are improperly (over)heard; content is inaudible; Prufrock's projected walk is through a world of other people's unintelligible conversations – 'muttering retreats' (l. 5), 'children whimpering in corners' ('Pervigilium', l. 5), streets where 'evil houses' 'Pointed a ribald finger at me in the darkness / Whispering all together, chuckled at me in the darkness' ('Pervigilium', ll. 16–17). Moreover, again temporarily leaving aside the identity of the inter-locutors, in the dialogue between 'You' and 'I', 'I' closes down 'You's' potential question: 'Oh do not ask, "What is it?"' (l. 11).

Prufrock's experience, therefore, is of less-than-ideal speech situations; admittedly, these are not all located in the public sphere and so might not be expected to result in communicative action. (The closing-down of participation, however, might explain why 'I' and 'You' fail to make any movement to 'go'.) In contrast, though the details are scanty, the projected tea-party does appear to constitute a public sphere. It is envis-aged as taking place in a space – a 'room' (ll. 13, 35) – which, although ostensibly part of someone's home and therefore private and domestic, is, for the life of the soirée, converted into a social venue. In this venue, conversation on non-personal subjects, if not explicit political critique, takes place. Nonetheless, an ideal speech situation still fails to obtain. Instead of rational interchange, there are 'formulated phrase[s]' (l. 56), digressions (l. 66), the desultory-sounding 'some talk of you and me' (l. 89), conversations to which interlocutors do not give their full atten-tion but are distracted by 'settling a pillow or throwing off a shawl, / And turning toward the window' (ll. 107–8). Far from open, egalitarian speech situations, Prufrock anticipates only barriers to communicative exchanges: inaudibility, misunderstanding, exclusivity.

'Talking of Michelangelo' deserves special mention. The women, coming and going, appear to be engaged in open debate; the repetition of the lines suggests an easy, fluent conversation. Is an ideal speech situation in progress within Prufrock's grasp? Habermas argues that the political public sphere was preceded by a 'literary public sphere', which was nonetheless 'political' because it was separate from the state;[25] the case is therefore made for an ideal speech situation comprising aesthetic discussion. But this must be qualified by Habermas's later comment that, in literary discourse:

> [T]he neutralization of the binding/bonding power frees the illocutionary acts (now robbed of their power) from the pressure to reach a decision which obtains in everyday communicative praxis; it removes them from the sphere of normal speech and reduces their role to that of the playful creation of new worlds – or, rather, to a pure demonstration of the world-disclosing power of innovative linguistic expressions.[26]

Discussion of literature – or works of art – might display the characteristics of ideal speech, but is released from the obligation of coordinating action. 'The women' may therefore be associated with an exclusive cultural elite of the type Habermas associates with the decline of the public sphere in late modernity.

Faced with these obstacles, it is unsurprising that Prufrock, in Eliot's construction, scarcely bothers to establish validity claims in support of his intended utterance. Given that the contents of this utterance are withheld in the poem, claims to truth and rightness do not offer themselves for analysis.[27] (Their absence, which points to a sense in Prufrock that objectivity and social norms are not worth petitioning, is nonetheless telling.) But Prufrock is preoccupied with the third kind of validity claim – to truthfulness. The thrust of his accumulated questions is: how will I be understood, believed, taken seriously? Any attempt he makes to establish his sincerity or authenticity will, he anticipates, be quickly negated as appraisals of his personal appearance undermine his authority: '(They will say: "How his hair is growing thin!")', '(They will say: "But how his arms and legs are thin!")' (ll. 41, 44). Hence, at the heart of the poem, is Prufrock's fear of communicative incompetence, both on his own part and on that of the 'one' whose response to rolling the universe towards 'some overwhelming question' (ll. 92–3) is, instead of 'say[ing] "yes" or "no" to [a] validity claim',[28] likely to be reiterated misunderstanding and contradiction: 'That is not what I meant at all. / That is not it, at all'; 'That is not it at all, / That is not what I meant, at all' (ll. 97–8, 109–10).

The ability to make and judge validity claims is dependent upon what Habermas calls a 'performative attitude':

> [A] speaker can in a performative attitude address himself to a hearer only under the condition that he learns to see and understand himself – against the background of others who are potentially present – from the perspective of his opposite number, just as the addressee for his part adopts the speaker's perspective for himself.[29]

this poem foreshadow Prufrockian panes (ll. 15, 16, 25), streets (ll. 4, 70) and windows (l. 72).

75. Ibid., p. 20. Again, there are a number of Prufrockian foreshadowings in this poem: 'gowns that fall from neck and knee' (l. 8) anticipate 'Arms that lie along a table', 'skirts that trail along the floor' (ll. 67, 102); the 'rich' sunset (l. 13) foreruns the 'necktie rich' (l. 43); 'And while one lifts her hand' (l. 14) looks forward to 'one, settling a pillow' (ll. 96, 107); 'porcelain, / Murmurs a word' (ll. 16–17) heralds 'Among the porcelain, among some talk of you and me' (l. 89).

76. Ibid., p. 26. In this poem, 'evenings [. . .] / That call, recall / So many nights and afternoons' (ll. 1, 6–8) foreshadow 'For I have known them all already, known them all / Have known the evenings' of 'Prufrock' (ll. 49–50).

77. Ibid., p. 28. Here, the 'cakes and tea' (l. 4) anticipate the 'tea and cakes and ices' in 'Prufrock' (l. 79); the 'eternal truths' the disturbance of the universe (l. 46); the 'silver spoon' (l. 6) the 'coffee spoons' (l. 51); the 'means and ways' (l. 19) the 'works and days' and 'days and ways' (ll. 29, 60).

78. Ibid., p. 70.

79. Henry James, *The Portrait of a Lady* (1880–1), ed. Geoffrey Moore (Harmondsworth: Penguin, 2003), p. 41.

80. Eliot, *The Complete Poems and Plays*, pp. 18–21, 31.

81. In the spring of 1914, Eliot attended a Sunday garden party held in Russell's honour by Professor Benjamin Fuller (MacCabe, *T. S. Eliot*, p. 24).

82. Harry T. Costello, *Josiah Royce's Seminar, 1913–14: As Recorded in the Notebooks of Harry T. Costello*, ed. Grover Smith (New Brunswick: Rutgers University Press, 1963), p. 85.

83. Quoted in Gray, *T. S. Eliot's Intellectual and Poetic Development 1909–1922*, p. 128.

84. T. S. Eliot, 'A Prediction in Regard to Three English Authors', *Vanity Fair* 21.6 (February 1924), pp. 29, 98: p. 29.

85. Cf. Eliot's comment in his introduction to the 1926 edition of *Savonarola*, a poem by his mother, Charlotte Eliot, referring to his earlier paper 'The Interpretation of Primitive Ritual': 'the same ritual remaining practically unchanged may assume different meanings for different generations of performers; and the rite may have originated before "meaning" meant anything at all'. T. S. Eliot, 'Introduction', in Charlotte Eliot, *Savonarola: A Dramatic Poem* (London: R. Cobden-Sanderson, 1926), pp. vii–xii: p. viii.

Chapter 3

Party Joyce: From the 'Dead' to When We 'Wake'

Jean-Michel Rabaté

> What is a 'party'? (1) *a partitioning*, isolating one group from another, (2) an orgy, or *partouze*, as we say in French, wherein the participants are linked erotically, and (3) a hand, or *partie*, the regulated moment in a game, a collective diversion. In Sade, in Fourier, the party, the highest form of societary or Sadian happiness, has this threefold character: it is a worldly ceremony, an erotic practice, a social act. (Roland Barthes, *Sade, Fourier, Loyola*)[1]

In the Hades episode of *Ulysses* (1922), Bloom and a group of acquaintances are sitting in a horse-drawn carriage that will take them to Prospect cemetery in Glasnevin. They are travelling together to bring their friend Dignam to his final rest. After a short while, they notice disquieting details. Martin Cunningham brushes some crumbs from under his thighs, and Mr Power avers: 'Someone seems to have been making a picnic party here lately.'[2] What follows provides one of the numerous narrative ellipses of this section:

> All raised their thighs and eyed with disfavour the mildewed buttonless leather of the seats. Mr Dedalus, twisting his nose, frowned downward and said:
> —Unless I am greatly mistaken . . . What do you think, Martin?
> —It struck me too, Martin Cunningham said.[. . .]
> Mr Dedalus sighed resignedly.
> —After all, he said, it's the most natural thing in the world. (U, p. 74)

Simon Dedalus's unexpressed thought is developed by Bloom a few pages later: 'Love among the tombstones. Romeo. Spice of pleasure. In the midst of death we are in life. Both ends meet. Tantalizing for the poor dead' (U, p. 89). Immediately after, Bloom remembers 'Molly wanting to do it at the window' (U, p. 89), a thought that will recur throughout the day. The fact that the funeral carriage has been rented by party-goers intent upon sexual pleasure, that for them food leads to sex whose traces are visible or smelly enough to be detected, will provide

a first context for the term of 'party' as used by Mr Power and also as I
see it underpinning Joyce's works. For Joyce, the term always connotes
sexual satisfaction and also entails a consideration of the organic opposites, since it tends to move from life to death and from death to life. We
understand why Bloom will be in mourning all day when he walks in the
streets of Dublin on 16 June 1904. He has to be dressed in black because
he would not want to 'Make a picnic of it' (U, pp. 46–7), yet this very
'picnic' (or 'party') redeems him for most readers at the end of novel.
I am alluding to the last pages, in which Molly Bloom concludes her
paean to life with a lyrical reenactment of their most meaningful kiss:
she passed him seedcake through her lips during a picnic on the Howth
promontory, and it was how she led him to propose to her. Thus, even
if we discover no 'party' as such in *Ulysses*, except in 'retrospective
arrangements', as in Molly's fond memories of Bloom's courtship, such
networks allow us to gain a crucial perspective on Joyce's entire works.
Indeed, one can say that Joyce's mature work stretches between two
parties: the memorably epiphanic party that functions as the setting
of 'The Dead' (1941), and the raunchy funeral wake that morphs and
polymorphs in and out of *Finnegans Wake* (1939). The relative scarcity
of party scenes in *Ulysses* should not detract from the fact that there is
a 'party' vector in Joyce's works. It would take us from the Christmas
dinner-party of *A Portrait of the Artist as a Young Man* (1916) to the
revelries of drinkers in a Chapelizod pub where most of *Finnegans Wake*
takes place, from the annual dance party at the Morkans in 'The Dead'
to the mythical 'wake' of Tim Finnegan. In all these, death lurks behind
the scenes, which explains why the main 'party' presented in *Ulysses* is
a group visit to a cemetery for a funeral. The Hades episode was to have
a momentous impact on two fellow modernists, T. S. Eliot and Ezra
Pound, who both felt inspired by Joyce to similar juxtapositions of life
and death via the theme of the ghost. But Joyce went on, weaving his
way through the complex ambivalence he always attached to the idea
of a 'party'. I will first examine how this idea plays out in 'The Dead'
before moving to *Finnegans Wake*.

A 'party' implies a sense of communal gathering for the most various
purposes, like birthdays, promotions, family visits, for the enjoyment of
a group of people who share certain beliefs and follow the same rituals.
One regular issue is: who can be invited to a party and who cannot? In
that sense, a party presupposes some form of hospitality.[3] This was a
feature of Dublin that Joyce felt he had not adequately represented in his
early stories, a 'hospitality' that led to a sense of communal festivity. By
comparison with other cities like London, Paris, Trieste or Zurich, one
can say that still today Dublin is defined by a rare openness to strangers.

The pleasure in revelry is allied to mutual exchange without immediate exploitation. A 'party' should embody this freedom from seduction or obligation. In 1906, Joyce wrote an often quoted letter to his brother Stanislaus in order to express this:

> Sometimes thinking of Ireland it seems to me that I have been unnecessarily harsh. I have reproduced (in *Dubliners* at least) none of the attraction of the city for I have never felt at my ease in any city since I left it except in Paris. I have not reproduced its ingenuous insularity and its hospitality. The latter 'virtue' so far as I can see does not exist elsewhere in Europe.[4]

His publisher, Grant Richards, had reproached Joyce for his censorious attitude when dealing with Dublin and the Irish. His stories would tend to denounce, debunk, criticise but never praise the city, shown as the epitome of betrayal, paralysis and corruption. Most of the *Dubliners* survive by exploiting weaker people. Irish values are all tainted by economic and moral prostitution.

Joyce's letter was mailed to his brother from Rome, where he was completing the original plan for his collection of short stories. The same letter expresses admiration for Arthur Griffith's nationalist political programme. The founder of Sinn Féin advocated then a total boycott of British goods, along with new educational schemes and a reformed national service; he planned the creation of a national banking system. There were only two attitudes that derived from the Sinn Féin nationalist programme to which Joyce objected – they had to do with race and language. Joyce refused anything that looked like sponsoring 'racial hatred', by which he meant the bigoted parochialism of the Irish, a provincialism that often veered into anti-Semitism, and he objected to the idea of using Gaelic as the national language of Ireland.

The pervasive nostalgia detectable in this letter was due to a certain culture shock experienced by Joyce during his Rome stay. It was while in Rome that he drafted *Exiles*, whose preparatory notes contain interesting allusions to a marital crisis, and planned 'The Dead', a late addition to *Dubliners* and a real turning-point in his career as a writer. True, writing 'The Dead' only partly fulfilled the task of 'making amends' for the rest of the stories, as Richard Ellmann showed in his biography.[5] The last story deals directly with the issue of hospitality in the context of a party. The plot hinges upon the speech that Gabriel is to deliver in order to thank his aunts for their annual dance and dinner. 'Hospitality' is the first of the headings reviewed when Gabriel rehearses his speech. 'He ran over the headings of his speech: Irish hospitality, sad memories, the Three Graces, Paris, the quotation from Browning.'[6] This outline is then modified after he has been taunted by Miss Ivors, whose brusque accusations upset his balance. Gabriel then decides to deflect the speech, so as to respond to her ironical remark that he is a 'West Briton':

> He would say, alluding to Aunt Kate and Aunt Julia: *Ladies and Gentlemen, the generation which is now on the wane among us may have had its faults but for my part I think it had certain qualities of hospitality, of humour, of humanity, which the new and very serious and hypereducated generation that is growing up around us seems to me to lack.* Very good: that was one for Miss Ivors. What did he care that his aunts were only two ignorant old women? (D, p. 193)

Among the multiple ironies that run parallel in these sentences, one can notice that it is the new militant tone that makes Gabriel change his quotation from Browning. Since he fears that it will sound too intellectual, he changes a 'thought-tormented music' into a 'thought-tormented age'. Gabriel's objective alliance with 'ignorant old women' he seems here to despise will be toned down during the actual performance: had he kept the phrase 'on the wane', he would have all too readily announced not only their disappearance but his own! The italicised paragraph expands into almost one page in the actual speech, in which Gabriel develops a contrast between what he perceives as the warm-hearted tradition needed by a true 'party' and a hyper-politicised and partisan attitude. Here, one can see how the 'party' is opposed to 'partisanship'. Gabriel prefers a humanist tradition to a one-sided nationalism since, for him, 'hospitality' becomes synonymous with a notion of general inclusiveness. The 'party' in his eyes is indeed a 'part for the whole'; this is the very synecdoche of this ancient 'hospitality'.

Yet, Gabriel's quandary becomes more obvious when we are privy to his erotic reveries. The image of universal harmony is indeed a dream he cherishes, but what triggers his deepest wish is the imagination of a renewed tryst with Gretta. What allows him to perform his public duties as head of the table, as the only male person in charge, is the thought that he will be alone with his wife at the end of the party. In fact, he needs to dream of a party for two only, in order to play the game of the social world. Gabriel's position will change considerably at the end of the story. Finally he will set out 'on his journey westward' (D, p. 225), if only metaphorically. He will try to understand better an unknown past linked with Irish values of which he had no notion, even when he was praising traditional values. Gabriel is too intelligent to be simply a smug 'praiser of the past', but his conservative humanism will not carry him very far. When he seems to be arguing for a truce between the warring factions, he leaves open the difficult question whether any 'party' – or literature, for that matter – can remain 'above politics' (D, p. 188).

The annual party arranged by the Morkan sisters is divided into two separate moments: first music and dancing, then a formal dinner. This family gathering becomes a 'party' since it includes a majority of friends, along with pupils of the three musical hostesses. We suspect that the date is that of the Epiphany, which should unite everyone, although the only precise period mentioned in the text is 'Christmas time'. 'Hospitality' functions not only as a synecdoche for the whole set of family values praised by Gabriel, but as a prompter for certain performances. A 'party' requires a performative, since the discourse of hospitality cannot be complete without its enactment. Gabriel will play the expected part, and provides the welcome or farewell speech that adds the ritual stamp. He will have then to harp on ancient values, confirming more than once that there are values that define the possibility of a 'party', and that they will endure. Thus, it is no wonder that Miss Ivors decides that she has to leave the house at once, in order to accept the dancing but not the dinner – and this puts Gabriel in an awkward position.

> Gabriel hesitated a moment and said:
> —If you will allow me, Miss Ivors, I'll see you home if you really are obliged to go.
> But Miss Ivors broke away from them.
> —I won't hear of it, she cried. For goodness sake go in to your suppers and don't mind me. I'm quite well able to take care of myself. (D, p. 196)

Her last words seem to rephrase ironically the Gaelic slogan for which she fights: *Sinn Féin amhain*, or 'ourselves alone'. Gabriel pretends to think that he is not the cause of her abrupt departure. At first, he had been anxious to find her among the audience but finds new confidence in the idea that he can berate her in her absence. All this suggests that Gabriel both wishes to exclude her from the gathering and to take her as an example of rudeness, of the brash new spirit he condemns. The hospitality of the party begins fissuring, since it needs an alien, a *xenos*, as a butt to satirise. The rejection of the other allows the party to rejoice in its fake universality. Gabriel is portrayed as the liberal intellectual who is caught up between values of the past that he cannot completely make his – there is a forced quality in his praise of tradition, which is visible in his use of pseudo-epic similes – and the growing militancy associated with a period of strife and impending trouble. Quite the Hegelian beautiful soul, Gabriel swoons too quickly, betraying his own alienation by recurrent sense of failure, his constant uneasiness.

Thus we understand that the hospitable party is fraught with tension and ambivalence. This is why Gabriel begins his speech with a bold image playfully suggesting victimisation: 'Ladies and Gentlemen. It is not the first time that we have gathered together under this hospitable roof, around this hospitable board. It is not the first time that we have been the recipients – or perhaps, I had better say, the victims – of the hospitality of certain good ladies' (D, p. 203). As anthropologists and explorers concur, the host is never far from the role of the sacrificial victim. The host is also a victim since he cannot refuse the consequences of an opening of privacy to strangers. The consequences can be momentous, as the example of Paris shows. Gabriel presents himself as Paris unable to choose between three goddesses or three graces: 'I will not attempt to play to-night the part that Paris played on another occasion. I will not attempt to choose between them. The task would be an invidious one and one beyond my poor powers' (D, p. 205). Symptomatically, Gabriel projects in this fantasy the very part he has played so far: someone who refuses to choose. However, refusing to choose is also a choice, but a wrong choice. Hence we see how Gabriel fails three times in his dealings with women. He fails with Lily, the caretaker's daughter, when he cursorily alludes to marriage and is 'discomposed by the girl's bitter and sudden retort' (D, p. 178). He also fails with Miss Ivors, by being brutal when she seems to enjoy his company; she teases him more out of admiration than rejection – she was, after all, inviting him and Gretta to a friendly group 'excursion' to the Aran islands. Another 'party' could have been constituted, a group of friends gathered by common values and a political ideal this time, but Gabriel refuses this opportunity. Finally, he fails when he misreads his wife's mood at the end. Thrilled by sexual desire, complacent about the possibility of a second honeymoon away from the children, he cannot imagine that she had experienced deeper love prior to their courtship. The regular discomfiture experienced by Gabriel can correspond to the goddesses among whom Paris had to choose. Hera, the goddess of marriage, could be invoked by Lily if only she had gone 'to her wedding' with a young man, instead of being betrayed (D, p. 177). Athena, the goddess of reason and also of politics, looks like Molly Ivors's tutelary divinity. Aphrodite, the goddess of love, must have looked the other way when Gretta obeyed her family's order and left Galway, thus condemning poor Michael Furey to an untimely death.

Gabriel's illusion of mastery is entirely destroyed when he senses that he appears pale and lame next to the image of a romantic youth who has braved death to say goodbye to a sweetheart. 'While he had been full of memories of their secret life together, full of tenderness of joy and desire, she had been comparing him in her mind with another. A shameful consciousness of his own person assailed him' (D, p. 221). At last, he sees himself as a 'nervous well-meaning sentimentalist' who was merely 'orating to vulgarians and idealising his own clownish lusts' (D, p. 221). As we know from *Ulysses*, a sentimentalist is defined by George Meredith, whom Stephen likes quoting, as someone who 'would enjoy without incurring the immense debtorship for a thing done' (U, pp. 550–1). This harsh definition is apt for Gabriel, who seems obsessed with tradition and pays homage to the rituals of old age. It captures the idealising mechanism that explains his attitude facing Gretta. In spite of his paralysing sense of secondariness, or perhaps because of it, Gabriel only pays lip-service to tradition. His escapism looks toward a modern Europe as a way out of his country's archaic feuds, which explains his desire to flee to France, Belgium or Germany. Just as he longs to be outside in the park full of snow when he mentally rehearses his speech, although we know that he habitually dreads the proximity of the snow and fears colds, he praises Irish hospitality at the same time as he confesses a distaste for his own country: 'O, to tell the truth, retorted Gabriel suddenly, I'm sick of my own country, sick of it!' (D, p. 190). Indeed, Gabriel praises what he betrays in thought and deed, flying away from Irish politics to go vacationing in Europe and writing for British newspapers that have more prestige than the local ones. There is an added dramatic irony in the fact that he praises the past just before being engulfed by a darker past coming from his wife's previous experiences with total strangers.

Concepts like 'party', 'hospitality' and 'exile' are never simple for Joyce and in particular in *Dubliners*. *Dubliners* is full of failed exiles, like Little Chandler or Bob Doran, who because they never find the courage to 'pay the price' finally opt for a slow inner death, and aborted parties as we see in 'Clay', when Maria fails to bring the peace she was hoping for. 'The Dead' dramatises in an eloquent and symphonic manner an idea that is developed by the celebrated Christmas dinner scene in *A Portrait of the Artist as a Young Man*. What the young Stephen Dedalus discovers is that a family party marked by repetitive rituals (it's his first admission to the table of the adults) cannot impose unity where there is strife and political infighting. The clash between Dante, who believes that the Catholic hierarchy has been right to reject Parnell because of his adultery, and Simon Dedalus and Mr Casey, who hold that Parnell's failure was due to the English, who cannily played up to religious prejudice, brings about an irreducible rift in the family's union. The constant tension between the ecumenism of the 'party' and the fractiousness of antagonistic political parties is recurrent in Joyce, and it should lead to a politicised reading of his texts.

Joyce was drafting 'The Dead' at a time when Lenin and his friends were promoting a different view of the party. This what brought Tom

evoked several times in *Finnegans Wake*, most obviously in the passage: 'Now I suggest to you that ere there was this plagueburrow, as you seem to call it, there was a burialbattell, the boat of million years. Would you bear me out in that, relatively speaking, with her jackstaff jerking at her pennyladders, why not, and sizing a fair sail, knowest thou the kind?' (FW, p. 479 ll. 24–8).

As O'Súilleabháin notices, the old wakes were merry affairs, social gatherings with games, music, singing, story-telling, pranks and a lot of drink and food. He even adds: 'They were far merrier than weddings.'[18] Thus the section on the 'night games' in II, 1, is replete with games that were performed at Irish wakes (the bulk of O'Súilleabháin's book is taken up by a long list of games).[19] They included guessing games, as in that episode, but more often games of strength and dexterity. The penalties for the losers could be severe: they ran the gamut from slapping to being pulled around the room by the ear.[20] Some participants ended up being maimed for life after a rough wake night. This explains why a whole section of O'Súilleabháin's book is devoted to mischief-making, horse-play, rough games, unruly behaviour and even general fighting at funeral wakes; given the excessive consumption of strong alcohol and the proximity of so many young men and women who had to stay for a whole night together, all sorts of excesses were observed. In many instances, potatoes, broken pipes, pepper, ashes, water, drink or clods of turf were thrown at the participants. Injuries, at times severe, were common. Woe to older people who would fall asleep by the corpse! They would wake up with their coats tied to the table, or with their beards shaved, even with their faces blackened by soot or polish.[21] The corpse was not spared from these sudden outbursts of communal violence. The table on which the body was displayed would often collapse, so that it would roll down to the floor. When the deceased had suffered from arthritis or rheumatism and the limbs had to be tied together for the presentation, it often happened that a trickster would cut the ropes, causing the corpse to sit up at once, which would terrify the other mourners. At times, the corpse itself was given a hand of cards so as to participate in various card games, a pipe was inserted into the mouth or it would be taken to the floor for a last posthumous dance.[22]

The wakes were also occasions for the settlement of political accounts. There are several accounts of how the Molly Maguires in the north of Ireland would go to wakes so as to make mischief and punish those who had refused to join them. The Fenians and the Cockades sought each other at wakes too.[23] This is why the Catholic clergy did all it could to stop the wakes, less for fear of the usual indecency, than in a wish to curb the bad blood generated between factions. But on the other hand, a good wake had to include some fighting. 'This is a sad day, when my father is put into the clay, and not even one blow struck at his funeral!' was a common saying.[24] On one level, no page of *Finnegans Wake* is without a reference to this ritualistic blending of farce and sorrow, of partying excessively and lugubriously keening for the dead. For instance, in one of the rare comments on his own text, Joyce explains in a letter to Harriett Weaver the multiple meanings of one title given to Anna Livia Plurabelle's 'manifesto': 'L'Arcs en His Ceiling Flee Chinx on the Flur' (FW, p. 104 ll. 13–14). Joyce explains that this alludes to the rainbow, to Noah's ark and to the old Irish king Roderick, but a fourth meaning is also provided: 'There is merriment above (larks) why should there not be high jinks below stairs?'[25] This alludes to the Chapelizod pub in which most of the action takes place. The term 'high jinks' captures well the noisy mix of childish merriment and pointed mischief-making that characterised the traditional Irish wake. The 'party' was a ritual and more than a ritual, since it provided the opportunity to settle bitter family or local feuds under the pretence of innocent gaming. In a similar manner, Joyce's life in Paris was marked by the ritual of birthday parties, celebrations of book publications and family weddings, at the end of which the Irish writer would launch into his personal adaptation of the Italian tarantella, his 'spider dance'. Those social ceremonies (to which one would be invited or not, as Samuel Beckett discovered when he was blamed for the incipient psychosis of Lucia Joyce) offered a fit accompaniment to the slow and painful birth of the *Wake*. The distant model was indeed the 'wake', the only 'party' that could not be ruined just because it had been planned as an anarchic event in advance.

In all this, we verify that *Finnegans Wake* anticipates Mikhail Bakhtin's vision of popular culture as harking back to a pagan pageant exhibiting an obscene body, a corpse coming alive so as to transcend the boundaries of life and death. Of course, by focusing on an Irish wake, Joyce implies all the mourners, and the 'body politic' of the mass of the Dubliners, are a great assemblage of drunk, fighting, slandering, copulating individuals. Even if this specific type of 'party' had long been judged too subversive by the Catholic Church, it has remained a defining feature of Ireland. When Joyce took the ballad of Finnegan as a point of departure, he not only went back to an archaic ritual specific to pre-Christian Celtic treatments of death, but jumped across centuries to present the modernity that lay there as well. He composed a polyphonic text made up of conflicting voices whose babelic din opposed any authoritative discourse. The party is called a 'hubbub caused in Edenborough' (FW, p. 29 ll. 35–6), which means more than a local allusion to the opposing quays of Eden and Burgh along the Liffey. This word is of Irish origin and means the 'loud noise made by a crowd'. New England colonists would apply it to some rambunctious games played by Native Americans. The party opens itself to the colonial other, and in doing so destroys the propriety of high decorum.

Bakhtin developed similar ideas in his monumental thesis devoted to Rabelais.[26] This he completed in 1946, definitively inserting literature into the context of a history of popular culture. Its main feature is an anarchic laughter that stems from the lower parts, including the scatological and the obscene. Thus the carnivalesque inversion of 'high' values will lead to an irresistible movement of affirmation and resistance. Both Joyce and Bakhtin evoke 'parties' so as to link experimental writing to a history of popular culture. The 'party' that Joyce keeps rewriting with slight variations in all his major works entails an embrace of death captured by a festive life teetering on the brink of excess. Beginning, as it were, with mourning, Joyce shows that merriment subsists through testimonies of bereavement, whereas sadness and discordant strife interfere in the midst of family gatherings. This is his roundabout way of coming as close as possible to the drive of all drives, Freud's death drive, a *Thanatos* without which one cannot be sure of feeling fully alive. Hence the sense that most readers have, that *Finnegans Wake* is a very sad book indeed. The mixture of moods ranges from the 'jovial' to the sad. Bruno's famous motto '*In tristitia hilaris, in hilaritate tristis*' ('cheerful in the midst of sadness, sad in the midst of cheerfulness') would thus remain fully valid for the later Joyce. All the while, he kept the notion that all his writing was just a game – to quote once more Barthes's threefold subdivision in the meaning of a 'party'. Didn't Joyce write those quietly despairing words to his old friend Harriet Weaver, once she had finally agreed to 'play' with him by giving 'orders' for the writing of certain texts? Joyce wrote: 'I know it is no more than a game but it is a game that I have learned to play in my own way. Children may just as well play as not. The ogre will come in any case.'[27] Readers may just as well play as not in Joyce's party – they won't regret it.

Notes

1. Roland Barthes, *Sade, Fourier, Loyola*, trans. Richard Miller (Berkeley: University of California Press, 1989), p. 111. I note that the original text (Paris: Seuil Points, 1971) keeps 'La party' as a title for this section. It is rare to see English words in Barthes's essays. The section begins with the question '*Qu'est-ce qu'une party?*' (p. 116). Barthes seems to think that a 'party' is an untranslatable idiom.
2. James Joyce, *Ulysses* (1918–20), ed. Hans Walter Gabler (New York:

Random House, 1986), p. 74. Hereafter page numbers are given in the text and denoted 'U'.

3. I have treated this topic in *James Joyce and the Politics of Egoism* (Cambridge: Cambridge University Press, 2001), pp. 153–60. I will cover some of the same ground in the following section, with a different emphasis.

4. *Letters of James Joyce*, ed. Stuart Gilbert and Richard Ellmann (New York: Viking, 1966), vol. 2, p. 166.

5. Richard Ellmann, *James Joyce*, rev. edn (Oxford: Oxford University Press, 1983), p. 245.

6. James Joyce, *Dubliners* (1914), ed. Terence Brown (New York: Penguin, 1992), p. 192. Hereafter page numbers are given in the text and denoted 'D'.

7. Tom Stoppard, *Travesties* (New York: Grove Press, 1975), pp. 58–9.

8. V. I. Lenin, 'Party Organisation and Party Literature' (1905), in *Collected Works* (Moscow: Progress Publishers, 1965), vol. 10, pp. 44–9.

9. Stoppard, *Travesties*, p. 57.

10. Ibid., p. 60.

11. Ibid., p. 58.

12. James Joyce, *Finnegans Wake* (London: Faber, 1939). Hereafter page numbers are given in the text and denoted 'FW'.

13. 'Games Issue', *Cabinet* 45 (spring 2012), pp. 100–3.

14. Seán O'Súilleabháin, *Irish Wake Amusements* (Dublin: Mercier Press, 1967).

15. See the section on 'Irish Ritual Cannibalism' in George Cinclair Gibson's excellent *Wake Rites: The Ancient Rituals of Finnegans Wake* (Gainesville: University Press of Florida, 2005), pp. 155–6.

16. See Lady Speranza Wilde, *Ancient Legends, Mystic Charms, and Superstitions of Ireland* (New York: Lemma, 1973), pp. 122–3; Gibson, *Wake Rites*, pp. 153–4.

17. O'Súilleabháin, *Irish Wake Amusements*, pp. 76–7.

18. Ibid., p. 26.

19. Ibid., pp. 75–129.

20. Ibid., pp. 49–52.

21. Ibid., p. 67.

22. Ibid., p. 67.

23. Ibid., p. 71.

24. Ibid., p. 72.

25. James Joyce, *Selected Letters*, ed. Richard Ellmann (London: Faber, 1975), p. 326.

26. Mikhail Bakhtin, *Rabelais and His World*, trans. Helene Iswolksy (Bloomington: Indiana University Press, 1984).

27. Letter of 16 October 1926 to Harriet Weaver, *Letters of James Joyce*, ed. Gilbert and Ellmann, vol. 3, p. 144.

wants to touch everything rather than admire it. The sensuous beauty of the scene is wrecked by crass consumption, and Sun stumps off wailing. The recurrent image of the nut handle focuses both Sun's attention and the reader's awareness of his shifting impressions; after the party 'Sun had never seen [his father] so jolly' (p. 172) but when Sun howls his father is 'no longer jolly' (p. 173). Both parents seem tipsy to the adult reader. The moment of disruption, like that of Frau Brechenmacher, is deeply felt by the protagonist but neither Sun nor the Frau can articulate it into an epiphanic revelation.

'Bliss', focused around a smaller dinner-party than 'Sun and Moon', is one of Mansfield's most enigmatic stories. The satirical element evident in 'Sunday Lunch' is in this story a thread within a subtly woven texture embracing ecstatic feeling, sensuous delight, erotic impulses and domestic detail. The playwright Eddie Warren, one of the guests, is a caricature:

> 'I *wonder* if you have seen Bilks' *new* poem called *Table d'Hôte*,' said Eddie softly. 'It's *so* wonderful. In the last Anthology. Have you got a copy? I'd *so* like to *show* it to you. It begins with an *incredibly* beautiful line: "Why Must it Always be Tomato Soup?"' (p. 185)

The clothes of the first three guests to arrive are also caricatured. Mrs Norman Knight, who is wearing an orange coat with black monkeys round the hem and up the front, 'did look like a very intelligent monkey – who had even made that yellow silk dress out of scraped banana skins. And her amber ear-rings; they were like little dangling nuts' (p. 179). Warren's white socks 'seem to have got so *much* whiter since the moon rose' (p. 179). The perceiving consciousness is that of the protagonist, Bertha, so she sees her baby as charming, not as grotesque, as do her guests: 'The baby had on a white flannel gown and a blue woollen jacket' (p. 175).

A third register is quite different; while her guests gossip about sexual liaisons Bertha herself is on the edge of experiencing the life of her body for the first time. She is in a heightened state of expectation, possibly of the sexual liberation that is the subject of party gossip: 'Why be given a body if you have to keep it shut up in a case like a rare, rare fiddle?' (p. 174). She seems to be searching intuitively through domestic objects for transcendence. She has bought purple grapes to tone in with the dining-room carpet and becomes almost hysterical at the success of her arrangement of the fruit bowl: 'For the dark table seemed to melt into the dusky light and the glass dish and the blue bowl to float in the air' (p. 175). In the same elevated state she looks at the garden:

> The windows of the drawing-room opened on to a balcony overlooking the garden. At the far end, against the wall, there was a tall, slender pear tree in fullest, richest bloom; it stood perfect, as though becalmed against the jade-green sky. Bertha couldn't help feeling, even from this distance, that it had not a single bud or a faded petal. Down below, in the garden beds, the red and yellow tulips, heavy with flowers, seemed to lean upon the dusk. A grey cat, dragging its belly, crept across the lawn, and a black one, its shadow, trailed after. (p. 178)

She sees 'the lovely pear tree with its wide open blossoms as a symbol of her own life' (p. 178) but the furtive sexuality of the cats, and the heavily sensuous red and yellow tulips against the perfect white blossom of the pear tree and the chilly jade-green sky may leave the reader with a different interpretation of this powerful visual image. When Bertha puts on a white dress with jade beads and green shoes and stockings she is enacting the bliss she feels, though the language of her interior monologue is the abrupt expression of an adolescent materialist rather than of a romantic modernist: 'Really – really – she had everything. She was young. Harry and she were as much in love as ever, and they got on splendidly and were really good pals' (p. 178). Friends, a dressmaker and a new cook who can make omelettes are included in her review of marital satisfaction; though the register is not overtly satirical, there is a disjunction between it and her ecstatic view of the slender pear tree.

When Pearl Fulton arrives, living up to her name in being 'all in silver, with a silver fillet binding her pale blond hair', her cool perfection regenerates Bertha's sensuous intoxication: 'What was there in the touch of that cool arm that could fan – fan – start blazing – blazing – the fire of bliss that Bertha did not know what to do with?' (p. 180). We are reminded that when they met at the club, 'Bertha had fallen in love with her, as she always did fall in love with beautiful women who had something strange about them' (p. 177), but she has no language with which to meditate on these homoerotic sensations. Instead she regards her guests as a decorative group in a play by Chekhov, and the reader has the sense that, as in plays by Chekhov, something bizarre and unexpected may happen. When Harry salivates and begins 'to glory in his "shameless passion for the white flesh of the lobster" and "the green of pistachio ices – green and cold like the eyelids of Egyptian dancers"' (p. 181), the reader wonders whether this is an oblique expression of desire for his wife, dressed as she is in white and green, or something closer to the physicality of the two cats. Bertha imagines that she has a moment of total rapport with Pearl Fulton as they gaze at the pear tree in the moonlight, reminiscent of Pearl's silver dress and her 'slender fingers that were so pale a light seemed to come from them' (p. 182). Now the tree 'seemed, like the flame of a candle, to stretch up, to point, to quiver in the bright air, to grow taller and taller as they gazed – almost to touch the rim of the round, silver moon' (pp. 182–3). Her experience of bliss suddenly precipitates Bertha into feeling ardent desire for her husband for the first time, though they were 'such good pals' (p. 184) that Bertha thinks her coldness has not mattered. The reader may disagree in view of Harry's lust for the white flesh of the lobster.

When Bertha glimpses her husband confirming what is evidently a regular assignation with Pearl Fulton, we realise why they both arrived late and why he has made a show of being rude to her. This provides a different take on the vision of the phallic pear tree stretching up to the round moon. Bertha's elevated discourse of the pear tree as a symbol of her life and of her affinity with Pearl disintegrates, and she seems to expect that her disillusionment will be mirrored in the tree:

> Bertha simply ran over to the long windows.
> 'Oh, what is going to happen now?' she cried.
> But the pear tree was as lovely as ever and as full of flower and as still.
> (p. 185)

Mansfield weaves her own tantalising cloth in this story, sustaining the satirical mode but intertwining it with conflicting registers. Again, the moment of disruption is clear to the reader as Bertha's conception of her bond with her husband and with Pearl is revealed to be an illusion, but Bertha herself has no language with which to articulate her misapprehension of her relationships. The contrast in the final lines between Bertha's restless longing for something momentous to happen and the tranquillity of the pear tree leaves the reader with a sharply etched but enigmatic image. Writing to Woolf, Mansfield referred to a letter from Chekhov in which he said that 'what the writer does is not so much to *solve* the question but to *put* the question. There must be the question put. That seems to me a very nice dividing line between the true & the false writer'.[39] 'Bliss' is evidence of Mansfield's subtle ability to put the question of whether Bertha has moved beyond her child-like bliss at the opening of the story to a more profound awareness of the pleasures and dangers inherent in sexual attraction.

All the stories discussed so far have a European setting. The last two parties to be considered are set in New Zealand and add a different dimension to Mansfield's ambition as a writer. She wrote in her journal in 1916: 'Oh, I want for one moment to make our undiscovered country leap into the eyes of the old world. It must be mysterious, as though floating – it must take the breath.'[40] The undiscovered country in these stories relates to hierarchies in a new world. Both focus on particular social situations and both use the perspective of a young girl; as always with Mansfield's stories, the reader is invited to guess the age of the protagonist. In 'Her First Ball', Leila's interior monologue swoops the readers in a cab with her Sheridan cousins towards her first dance, sharing her observations about their magical appearance: 'Meg's tuberoses, Jose's long loop of amber, Laura's little dark head, pushing above her white fur like a flower through snow' (p. 265). The text itself seems to be in movement as Leila registers details in passing: 'on the pavement gay couples seemed to float through the air; little satin shoes chased each other like birds' (p. 265). She may be too excited to notice a paradoxical appeal in the ladies' room: '"Aren't there any invisible hair-pins?" cried a voice. "How most extraordinary! I can't see a single invisible hair-pin"' (p. 266).

It is clear from the beginning of the story that Leila is from an isolated and remote country home, and had tried to get out of coming to the ball but now 'the rush of longing she had had to be sitting on the verandah of their forsaken up-country home, listening to the baby owls crying "More Pork" in the moonlight, was changed to a rush of joy so sweet that it was hard to bear alone' (pp. 266–7). The story is rooted in its setting. When Leila dances with 'quite an old man – fat, with a big bald patch on his head' (p. 267), whose 'waistcoat was creased, there was a button off his glove, his coat looked as if it was dusty with French chalk' (p. 269), her astute sartorial assessment of him does not prepare her for his ability to shatter the magic of the moment. She has pitied his age and he retaliates by saying that before long she will be one of the chaperones 'sitting up there on the stage, looking on, in your nice black velvet. And these pretty arms will have turned into little short fat ones' (p. 269). Leila stops dancing because she 'wanted to be at home, or sitting on the verandah listening to those baby owls' (p. 270). Another partner comes along and once again the 'lights, the azaleas, the dresses, the pink faces, the velvet chairs, all became one beautiful flying wheel' (p. 270). On this occasion the moment of disturbance may register more decisively with the reader than with the character. Leila doesn't recognise the fat man when she bumps into him with a new partner, but he punctures the reader's image of the ball. The deft depiction of New Zealand life, with its respectable chaperones and narrow social round ('Were you at the Neaves' on Tuesday?' (p. 269)), also sketches in a different, non-European landscape with its own wildlife in which the young, like Leila, come to consciousness.

That issue is of particular relevance to the final story in the sequence, 'The Garden Party'. The story was first published over three weeks in the *Westminster Gazette* and, as McDonnell explains, significant passages were deleted:

Chapter 5

Virginia Woolf's Idea of a Party

Bryony Randall

The rhythm of Virginia Woolf's daily existence in early adulthood was largely dictated by the social obligations of a young English woman of her class, a round of activities including regular attendance at, and hosting of, a variety of different parties. Lunch- and tea-parties she often found simply dull; evening-parties, however, were much more difficult for both Woolf and her sister Vanessa. It was not only that the young women frequently felt awkward and out of place at such events (in a diary entry for 15 July 1903, Virginia claims that she and Vanessa frequently spoke to no-one for an entire evening).[1] Their chaperoning by their half-brother George, and his proprietorial attitude towards them (inspecting and criticising their choice of clothes, berating them for perceived failures to behave appropriately), made the whole experience of party-going fraught with potential distress – and, ultimately, danger. Woolf's memoir '22 Hyde Park Gate' is largely taken up with the description of her first evening-party escorted by George; not only did she return home weary and disappointed, but once she had retired to bed, George entered her room, 'flung himself on my bed, and took me in his arms' – he was, she records, both her and Vanessa's 'lover'.[2] 'Old Bloomsbury' picks up where '22 Hyde Park Gate' leaves off, and here there is a significant slippage in narrative tense, for while Woolf begins by recalling the specific party described in the previous piece, she then states that 'There would be a tap at the door; the light would be turned out and George would fling himself on my bed, cuddling and kissing and otherwise embracing me.'[3] The verb form confirms that sexual abuse at the hands of her half-brother following attendance at a party was not an exceptional event. In sum, it is not surprising that there is little in the record of Woolf's early years evincing enthusiasm for parties of any hue.

In later years, Woolf displayed at least a more ambivalent attitude towards parties, as her husband recalled (reflecting here on the period 1920–23 in particular):

Virginia loved 'Society', its functions and parties, the bigger the better; but she also liked – at any rate in prospect – any party. Her attitude to this, as to most things, was by no means simple. The idea of a party always excited her, and in practice she was very sensitive to the actual mental and physical excitement of the party itself, the rise of temperature of mind and body, the ferment and fountain of noise. Sometimes she enjoyed it as much in the event as in anticipation, and sometimes, of course, owing to her peculiar vulnerability to the slings and arrows of (not very) outrageous fortune, she would leave a boring party in despair as if it were the last scene of Wagner's Götterdämmerung with Hogarth House and the universe falling in flames and ruin about her ears. [. . .] She not only enjoyed society, the kaleidoscope of human beings, conversation, and the excitement of parties, she was through and through a professional novelist, and all this was the raw material of her trade.[4]

The diaries and letters of Woolf's mature years certainly record frequent and sometimes rapid shifts in attitude towards parties, between enjoyment and temporary, or supposedly permanent, avowals of renunciation. Indeed, they suggest a rather more negative attitude to parties than Leonard's recollection offers. For example, in a letter to Marjorie Joad (the Woolfs' assistant at the Hogarth Press) dated July 1924, Woolf insists that, while 'it was great fun at the party [held by John Maynard Keynes], enchanting, lyrical, Shakespeare with not a coarse word, and chaste conversations everywhere', she now 'do[esn't] want any more parties for an age, but to live like a caterpillar on a leaf'.[5] Six months later, however, she agreed to co-host a party with her sister-in-law Karin Stephen but, rather than anticipating it with pleasure, her letters of invitation record nothing but dread, referring to it as 'an awful, awful, awful party' and 'an appalling party'.[6] In the event, illness meant that she was unable to attend; or, as the case may be, 'illness gave her the excuse to miss [. . .] the party'.[7] An oscillating pattern of sociability and withdrawal was in part informed over the years by her physical movement between London, Richmond and Sussex, as well as the state of her health. But it was also connected to the pattern of her writing. And it is here that we can start to detect a more intimate relationship between parties and Woolf's creative output; namely, one very productive way of seeing the relationship between her texts is as that between guests at a party. My aim here is gradually to move towards this suggestion, through analyses of the ways in which Woolf represents parties and talks about them in her diaries and letters.

An apparent incompatibility between parties, or at least certain kinds of parties, and Woolf's ability to write is vividly expressed in her diary entry for 22 October 1935, composed while Woolf was in the closing stages of working on *The Years* (1937):

to the clothes they have, presumably, carefully selected for this event); Eleanor 'stopped'; '[a]gain the music interrupted'; she 'stopped' again; and eventually '[t]he music stopped [. . .] the couples broke apart'.[25] The stratification brought into play by Peggy's position on the floor, as she experiences the physical layers of the party, resonates with the concept of 'inconsecutive conversations' to encourage us to read the party vertically as well as horizontally, as the meaning of conversations proceeds not just, or even not at all, in a linear, consecutive fashion.

There is critical precedent for viewing conversation as a significant theoretical tool through which to examine Woolf's texts, and her party texts in particular. Anne Besnault-Levita has described Woolf's party stories of 1925 as 'built around the idea of conversation as a form of social exchange'.[26] She clarifies, however, that here it is the failure of communication, as much as, indeed more than, its success, with which Woolf is particularly concerned. At the same time, conversation has, for Woolf, 'a political as well as an ethical value', understood not just to mean that it bears ideological weight, as it clearly does, but also to mean that conversation can be valuable; it can act as a positive model of interaction.[27] I want to explore the possibilities that the representation specifically of those 'inconsecutive conversations' generated by the party space, which disrupt social, narrative or formal expectations, offers, both in readings of specific texts by Woolf and, ultimately, to inform an understanding of the relationships between her texts.

The idea of the inconsecutive conversation appears at a significant moment in one of Woolf's earliest fictional writings, the short story 'Phyllis and Rosamond' (1906). This text describes the experience of the two sisters Hibbert, closely resembling Woolf and Vanessa as young women, whose stifling social lives and attitudes are, briefly, challenged by their attendance, unchaperoned, at a party given by the Tristrams, who live in a 'distant and unfashionable quarter of London' – namely Bloomsbury (where the Stephen siblings had in fact moved from Kensington two years previously).[28] The Tristrams are clearly modern in a way that Phyllis and Rosamond are not, in their attitudes to religion, love, marriage and art. The intensity of the conversations that take place at this party are highly disconcerting to the sisters, and at one point Rosamond is 'surprised to find that her most profound discoveries were taken as the starting point of further investigations, and represented no conclusions'.[29] It is useful here to note that the *OED* defines 'inconsecutive' as 'characterized by want of sequence'.[30] Here, what the sisters assume to be the normal sequence of conversation, including what marks the beginning, middle and end of these social interactions, is disrupted. Thus, while the conversations recorded are, by comparison with those at the party in *The Years*, entirely coherent, to this extent they are 'inconsecutive' to the Hibberts; they do not follow the familiar sequence of remarks, governed by conservative social norms, which hitherto constituted, for these young women, party conversation.

Woolf's later texts move, however, from a description of the disruption of expected sequences generated by a clash of social expectations, to formal evocations of inconsecutive party conversation. The years 1918–22 saw Woolf produce some of the most formally experimental of all her texts, mainly in the form of short stories, but where this experimentation found its way into her novels it was not, apparently, universally acclaimed. So, for example, Woolf's diary entry for 26 July 1922 records Leonard's rapturous reception of *Jacob's Room* – '[h]e calls it a work of genius' and 'without lapse (save perhaps the party)'.[31] This tantalising caveat is not explained; we do not know what it is about the party which Leonard sees as falling short of the otherwise 'interesting [. . .] beautiful [. . .] quite intelligible' novel. But perhaps it is in this last regard that Leonard identified the 'lapse'. The party chapter of *Jacob's Room* (chapter 7) is approached particularly obliquely, even in this novel of oblique approaches, via a description of the vogue for paper flowers used to decorate finger-bowls. The main part of the chapter is made up of a series of interrupted dialogues, or rather fragments of speech, only some of which appear to describe successful communication. Characters frequently interrupt themselves, and each other; and the narrative also interrupts one dialogue to launch with no explanation into a conversation between other characters, some of whom are already familiar to the reader, some of whom appear only this once.[32] The fragmentary nature of the conversations is emphasised by the use of white space to separate short pieces of text from each other. If, as Julia Eliot says, '"the amusing thing about a party is to watch the people – coming and going, coming and going"',[33] then there is certainly plenty of opportunity for this pastime at this particular party; indeed, there is little other than 'coming and going'. The form of this party scene puts the reader in Julia's position; the lack of sequence or explanation between the snippets of conversation offers the reader a sense of both excitement and confusion.

Both these qualities, evoked by 'inconsecutive conversations', are particularly prominent in the experience of reading Woolf's apparently unfinished short story 'The Evening Party'. Woolf toyed with the idea of calling this piece 'A Conversation Party', drawing yet further attention to its defining characteristic. It was apparently first drafted in 1918, revisited in 1921 (when Woolf was working on both *Jacob's Room* and what was to become the short story collection *Monday or Tuesday*), and possibly also revisited in 1925, around the time the later party short stories were drafted.[34] It is at this later date that she described an idea for a story made up of 'an exciting conversation all, or almost all, in dialogue', which, as Susan Dick speculates, 'may also refer to this story', eventually published in Dick's collection as 'The Evening Party'.[35] Save the first two paragraphs, the story is indeed made up entirely of dialogue. It is similar in this respect to the party scene in *Jacob's Room*, which is also made up mostly of direct speech but which, unlike 'The Evening Party', contains some connective commentary.[36] 'The Evening Party' begins by setting the kind of glamorous, inviting scene that might be expected with 'the idea of a party': 'sweet is the night air' in the street, we are told by the first-person narrator as he or she approaches 'the house of the party'; 'the tree droops its dark shower of blossom'; inside the house, '[o]n every chair there is a little soft mound; pale whisps of gauze are curled upon bright silks'; and 'in [the] faces [of the other guests] the stars seem to shine through rose coloured flesh'.[37] There is none of the awkwardness, anxiety or disillusionment that pervades the later party stories; while one of the speaking voices observes that the other party guests 'don't exist',[38] this is mild condemnation, and apparently of no concern (the narrator and his or her companion continue their poetic exchange with reflections on Shelley and Blake), in contrast to the disapproval, confusion or outright hostility generated in protagonists by their fellow guests in the later party stories. The atmosphere of elegance and decorousness pervades the story throughout, to the final lines: 'The lights rise and fall; the water's thin as air; the moon's behind it. D'you sink? D'you rise? D'you see the islands? Alone with me.'[39]

The conversations which take place here do not have the self-censoring, halting aspect of the conversation in *The Years*, nor are they physically disjointed from each other (in terms of both space on the page and space within the imagined party) as in *Jacob's Room*. Indeed, in some parts they appear just as 'consecutive' as the conversations in, for example, 'Phyllis and Rosamund'. Rather, they are 'inconsecutive' insofar as they either lack logical sequence, frequently following an aesthetic and/or intimately personal line, which the reader can only infer rather than having it explained by any narrative description of interiority (as in the later party stories); or because, when a new speaker joins the two central voices, there is none of the usual narrative paraphernalia alerting us to this shift in dynamic – that is, we are not told who is speaking. Therefore, when Dominic Head asserts that 'the exploration by the narrator of impressions received is interrupted by other guests at the party whose collective conversation betrays a restricted outlook',[40] the word 'interrupted' is to some extent inaccurate. The central conversation between narrator and companion might indeed have continued along different lines if, for example, one of them had not spotted the professor 'loom[ing] upon us', or at another moment if the hostess had not overheard 'talk of melancholy at my party?'[41] (surely prefiguring Mrs Dalloway's distress that 'in the middle of my party, here's death').[42] Head's reading of the text identifies a tension between the inclusivity proposed by the main speaker and the hierarchising approach of the professor of literature with whom (s)he discusses the merits of both the 'moderns' and the 'ancients'. Such a 'restricted outlook' could also be imputed to the party guest who admires the main speaker's writing; and the other who remembers him or her as a child. Yet the extent to which these interactions can be read as interruptions is almost entirely mitigated by the smooth textual surface of the story, eschewing entirely any indirect discourse, regardless of who is speaking. The opening utterances of new characters are not at all, to this extent, experienced by the reader as 'interruptions' – the already 'inconsecutive' conversation continues, paradoxically without stylistic break or rupture. Head's reading ultimately relies on an interpretation of the content of these interactions, failing to give significant weight to the formal qualities of this text in this regard.

The form of this text raises the question of what counts as, and who defines, 'consecutive' conversation. Head's reading insists that the other party guests disrupt the sequence of the conversation between the two main voices. But is it not precisely the point of a party that interactions occur which may challenge or distract – and in so doing may indeed offer otherwise unforeseen opportunities (as when, for example, we hear more about the narrator's views on literary history in his or her interaction with the professor)? This is the risk one takes when attending a party. The fact that, in this story, it is often difficult even to identify which of the supposedly separate characters is speaking, on the one hand, evokes the mingling of voices at a noisy party, but, on the other, implies a welcoming of all voices at the same level of narrative discourse. These interactions are as much a part of the narrator's experience of this party as his or her 'poetic flight'.[43] The party space, in principle at least, is a non-hierarchical one, where bodies can move and voices interact freely, and with the same level of authority. In practice, the power imbalances of the wider social world – based on gender, class, education, or wealth – do infiltrate the party space (as critics such as Besnault-Levita, Skrbic, Christine Reynier and Beth Rigel Daugherty argue). But the flattening of hierarchy in the consistently inconsecutive form of 'The Evening Party' reminds the reader of the different-but-equal premise of the very 'idea of a party'.

Inconsecutive conversations, then, while not necessarily offered by

Woolf in every instance as ideal models of interaction, at least have the great advantage of reflecting the non-hierarchical party space, which in turn provides a model for the non-hierarchical relationship I am proposing between Woolf's texts. What is more, if they are 'characterized by want of sequence', then they clearly resonate with her celebrated programme for a progressive woman's writing in *A Room of One's Own* (1929).[44] The profitability of a broken sequence, yet one in productive tension with the search for, or 'want of', such continuity or cohesion, takes us to my proposition that the party might offer us a model for the relationship between Woolf's texts. In the period between Woolf's first draft of 'The Evening Party' and her return to it, she made a now well known diary entry (dated 26 January 1920) which explicitly points towards a party model for the relationship between her texts: '[C]onceive [?],' she suggests, 'mark on the wall, K[ew]. G[ardens]. & unwritten novel taking hands & dancing in unity'.[45] Once again, this image of a literary form made up of a collection of otherwise discrete texts ('The Mark on the Wall' and 'Kew Gardens' are names of short stories Woolf had recently written) led her towards her next novel, *Jacob's Room*. But the terms she uses here explicitly evoke the image of the party (albeit a dance-party, a type of which she herself seemed not particularly fond). Critics have tended to focus here on Woolf's search for 'a "unity" in this form',[46] both in terms of its being a particular feature of the short story (Head's Bakhtinian analysis, positing the short-story genre as participating more closely in poetic discourse than the novel and the form thus pulling in the direction of a 'unitary' poetic language)[47] and in analyses of the short-story cycle (Skrbic's use of short-story theory to emphasise the 'harmony [. . .] the unalterable and permanent' informing 'the Mrs Dalloway grouping').[48] Certainly Woolf envisages an eventual 'unity', but excessive critical emphasis on this aspect means that the 'dancing' here gets lost. What Woolf seems to imagine is a space where (textual) bodies move together and apart, constantly, creating different configurations as they come into contact with each other at different moments. This offers a highly productive model for reading not only Woolf's party texts, but her works as a whole. A powerful means of guarding against hierarchisation is movement – hence the semi-paradox of 'dancing' in 'unity'. The party space, though potentially oppressive, at least offers in principle the opportunity to move, change perspective.

One can see this in, for example, Daugherty's ample – one can never say comprehensive – mapping of the links both between these party short stories, and with *Mrs Dalloway* and *To The Lighthouse*. Daugherty comes to no final conclusions about the relationship between these texts, but emphasises the different light shed on them when viewed in different configurations, offering the suggestion that these short stories in particular appear as a place of 'process', with all the connotations of ongoing movement and dynamism that this term involves.[49] But there are further connections that can be read between, in this case, the party short stories and other texts from other periods in Woolf's career. So, for example, the scene discussed above from the party in *The Years* where Peggy contemplates a book in solitude resonates strongly with 'The New Dress', where Mabel, alone at Mrs Dalloway's party, berates herself for looking at a picture 'from shame, from humiliation': 'As if one went to a party to look at a picture!'[50] Compare also Peggy's later assertion that 'I do not love my kind'[51] with the party story 'The Man Who Loved His Kind', featuring two individuals who both assert that they 'love their kind' yet conclude their conversation '[h]ating each other, hating the whole houseful of people'.[52] Peggy's self-scrutiny here – 'Was she not seeing herself in the becoming attitude of one who points to his bleeding heart?'[53] – casts her as a more self-aware, thus more modest and sympathetic, version of Prickett Ellis of 'The Man Who Loved His Kind'; the re-gendered pronoun amplifies this connection. These 'dances' between texts, imagining them as party-guests mingling in a space which offers both structure and freedom, open onto new possible readings of each, without proffering either as a definitive gloss on the other.

The idea of Woolf as hostess of a textual party is given further weight by the fact that she wonders whether she is 'sufficiently mistress of things' to achieve the new literary form she envisages. The locution could point in a number of directions but, read in context, emerging from reference to 'a gaiety – an inconsequence – a light spirited stepping at my sweet will',[54] which resolves into the image of 'dancing' texts, one cannot help but imagine Woolf here as mistress of a house, hosting a party where these texts will dance, in light-spirited steps. It is with this image, of the writer as hostess (and the hostess as creative force), that this discussion will conclude.

The writer as hostess

Woolf's genuine admiration of the successful hostess is implied in her description of her lover, Vita Sackville-West: 'I rather marvel at her skill, & sensibility, for is she not mother, wife, great lady, hostess, as well as scribbling?'[55] Woolf's feeling about hosting parties was, as we have seen, apt to 'weigh [. . . her] down with horror',[56] but, perhaps particularly for this reason, she admired, as well as satirised, the successful hostess. For example, Woolf's 1936 memoir 'Am I a Snob?' focuses on her friend-

46. Clare Hanson, *Short Stories and Short Fiction, 1880–1980* (London: Macmillan, 1985), p. 66.
47. Head, *The Modernist Short Story*, p. 96.
48. Skrbic, *Wild Outbursts of Freedom*, p. 152.
49. Beth Rigel Daugherty, '"A corridor leading from Mrs. Dalloway to a new book": Transforming Stories, Bending Genres', in Kathryn N. Benzel and Ruth Hoberman (eds), *Trespassing Boundaries: Virginia Woolf's Short Fiction* (New York: Palgrave Macmillan, 2004), pp. 101–24: p. 109.
50. Woolf, *The Complete Shorter Fiction*, p. 173.
51. Woolf, *The Years*, p. 312.
52. Woolf, *The Complete Shorter Fiction*, p. 200.
53. Woolf, *The Years*, p. 312.
54. Woolf, *Diary*, vol. 2, p. 14.
55. Ibid., p. 313.
56. Woolf, *Letters Vol. III*, p. 159.
57. Virginia Woolf, 'Am I a Snob?', in *Moments of Being*, pp. 204–20: p. 212.
58. Woolf, *Diary*, vol. 3, p. 12.
59. Indeed, in her 1923 essay 'Mr Bennett and Mrs Brown', Woolf explicitly draws an analogy between hostess and writer: 'Both in life and in literature it is necessary to have some means of bridging the gulf between the hostess and her unknown guest on the one hand, the writer and his [sic] unknown reader on the other'. Virginia Woolf, *Collected Essays*, ed. Leonard Woolf (London: Hogarth Press, 1966), vol. 1, pp. 319–37: pp. 330–1. Lorraine Sim argues that '"Mr Bennett and Mrs Brown" presents the ordinary as the basis for an ethics of intimacy', and this intimacy is effected through Woolf's 'play[ing] the part of "hostess" to her reader'. Lorraine Sim, *Virginia Woolf: The Patterns of Ordinary Experience* (Farnham: Ashgate, 2010), p. 185.
60. Woolf, *Diary*, vol. 3, p. 32.
61. Woolf, *Mrs Dalloway*, pp. 8, 67.
62. Other of Woolf's hostesses are also aware of their creative role – see for example Mrs Ramsay's aesthetic appreciation of the arrangement of the fruit bowl on the dinner table, which is both part of, and a metaphor for, the dinner she hosts. Virginia Woolf, *To The Lighthouse* (1927) (London: Penguin, 1992), pp. 105–6.
63. She quotes frequently to herself from *Cymbeline*, and her bedtime reading is the far from low-brow 'Baron Marbot's *Memoirs*'. Woolf, *Mrs Dalloway*, pp. 10, 32, 43, 204; 34–5.
64. Adam Barrows, *The Cosmic Time of Empire: Modern Britain and World Literature* (Berkeley: University of California Press, 2011), pp. 126–7.
65. Virginia Woolf, *The Waves* (1931) (London: Penguin, 1992), p. 95.
66. Woolf, *Mrs Dalloway*, p. 4.
67. Ibid., p. 5.
68. Reynier, *Virginia Woolf's Ethics of the Short Story*, pp. 14–15.
69. Anna Snaith, *Virginia Woolf: Public and Private Negotiations* (Basingstoke: Palgrave Macmillan, 2000), p. 4.

Chapter 6

Proustian Peristalsis: Parties Before, During and After

David R. Ellison

> The nature of parties has been imperfectly studied. It is, however, generally understood that a party has a pathology, that it is a kind of an individual and that it is likely to be a very perverse individual. And it is also generally understood that a party hardly ever goes the way it is planned or intended. This last, of course, excludes those dismal slave parties whipped and controlled and dominated, given by ogreish professional hostesses. These are not parties at all but acts and demonstrations, about as spontaneous as peristalsis and as interesting as its end product. (John Steinbeck, *Cannery Row*)[1]

The reader might wonder whether John Steinbeck's amusing statement on 'the nature of parties' applies exclusively to the novel in which it appears, or whether it has a broader applicability. *Cannery Row* (1945), set in Monterey, California, during the Great Depression, is a concatenation of short scenes tied together by two parties – one which takes place about halfway through the book, and which is disastrous in its results, and a second one, which is planned as an act of atonement for the first one. A group of unemployed or underemployed men usually referred to as 'The Boys' by the narrator decide to throw a party for one of the book's main characters, a marine biologist called Doc, who has been good to them over the years. The first party's origin has an ethical dimension. The idea is to redeem, in one grand gesture, a debt that has been incurred over time. In the eyes of the party's organisers, the surprise element, or, in Steinbeck's language, its 'spontaneous' character, is crucial (though, in the novel, spontaneity leads to chaos and to destruction, much to Doc's chagrin). In fact, according to the theory expressed in the quoted passage, the authentic party is spontaneous, whereas the inauthentic party is put together by 'ogreish professional hostesses' who whip and control and dominate the cast of characters they have invited. This kind of event is really not a party at all, Steinbeck writes, but an 'act' or a 'demonstration' resembling nothing so much as *peristalsis*. A humorous comparison indeed, but could it be that Steinbeck's humour, like that of Marcel Proust, says much more than it appears to say? And could it be that, despite the obvious differences between Steinbeck's concise Depression-era story and Proust's epic set in the upper echelons of Third Republic French high society, the American writer's theory of parties might have a certain strong, albeit covert, applicability to Proust's imaginary universe? I should like to examine this possibility; but to do so, it is first necessary to dwell a little longer with Steinbeck and with the peculiar use of the digestive metaphor with which he concludes his remarks.

The dictionary definition of *peristalsis* (a medical term which derives from the Greek *peri*, around, and *stellein*, to place) is: 'the rhythmic, wavelike motion of the walls of the alimentary canal and certain other hollow organs, consisting of alternate muscular contractions and dilations that move the contents of the tube onward'.[2] The conflation of the controlled, non-spontaneous party with the regularity of the digestive process culminating in a bowel movement provides the passage with a fine 'evacuative' terminus, but it is also perhaps more Proustian, more seriously Proustian, than it initially appears. The reader of *À la recherche du temps perdu* (*In Search of Lost Time*, 1913–27)[3] knows that most of the parties staged in the novel are far from spontaneous. In fact, the quintessential Proustian hostess, Mme Verdurin, who presides over the *petit clan* (little clan, little group) to which Swann gains access in his pursuit of Odette, could easily be described as 'ogreish', dominating and controlling. The psychological paradigm of sado-masochism functions throughout the *Recherche*, and is especially evident in the social scenes, even those scenes which seem frivolous and based upon snobbism and verbal jousting.

The one over-riding law of human social intercourse in Proust is the rigid dichotomy of inclusion versus exclusion. Indeed, if there is a narrative rhythm in the intercalated novella 'A Love of Swann's' (a 300-page third-person narrative which Proust inserted into the middle of the novel's first volume, *The Way by Swann's*), it is provided by this dichotomy. Initially indifferent to the charms of Odette de Crécy, Swann meets her in the Verdurin salon, falls in love with her as he becomes included in the salon, becomes jealous of her as she begins an affair with another man, is excluded from the salon, then falls out of love. The initial Stendhalian *crystallisation*[4] and final disenchantment of the love experience are conveyed, narratively, by the alternating rhythms of inclusion and exclusion. Exclusion is a kind of elimination; Proustian *peristalsis* occurs as individual characters in the novel move through the gradations of the social structure and are expelled from it.[5]

Like Steinbeck, Proust is not averse to alluding to, and developing at some length, the metaphor of digestion/elimination, in some cases with comic brio. In one ironically turned scene, Proust depicts one of the novel's most ambitious society matrons, Mme de Saint-Euverte (a lady who uses the parties of others to recruit for her own social functions), as the butt of a scatological diatribe by the Baron de Charlus. Here, a person whose function it is to include and exclude people from her salon is herself 'expelled' by Charlus, one of the novel's best-developed and most outrageous characters. In his conversation with the young narrator, Charlus opens the floodgates:

> Would you believe that this impertinent young man, he [Charlus] said, indicating me to Mme de Surgis, has just asked me, with none of the care one ought to take to hide these sorts of needs, whether I was going to Mme de Saint-Euverte's, that is, I fancy, whether I had the colic. I should attempt in any case to relieve myself in some more comfortable spot than at the house of someone who, if memory serves, was celebrating her centenary when I was making my entry into society, i.e., not *chez elle*. Yet who would be more interesting to listen to than her? So many historical memories, seen or lived through, from the days of the First Empire and the Restoration, so many intimate stories, too, with nothing 'Saint-ly' about them for sure but must have been very '*vertes*',[6] to judge by how she still frisks about on those venerable hams! What would stop me from interrogating her about those exciting times is the sensitivity of my olfactory apparatus. Mere proximity to the lady is enough. I suddenly say to myself: 'Oh, good God, someone's burst my cesspit', but it's simply that the Marquise, with the aim of getting some invitation, has just opened her mouth. (*In Search of Lost Time*, vol. 4, pp. 104–5)

Beyond Proust's more than occasional resorting to scatological wordplay, there is another sense in which the metaphorical use of *peristalsis* may be of help to the reader of the *Recherche* in his or her efforts to grasp the novel's narrative organisation. If we return to the etymological origins of the term (*peri*, around, and *stellein*, to place), I shall be suggesting, in the following development, that the Proustian narrative 'flow' can be aptly characterised by the pressure exerted by a narrative frame on the scene (here, the party scene) it encloses. Although it is true that a number of the minutely detailed party scenes in the novel appear as self-contained set-pieces, several of them are either preceded or followed by shorter episodes of quite extraordinary significance to the overall thematic arsenal of the *Recherche*. These shorter episodes exert pressure on the party scenes and tend to overshadow or undercut them in various ways. A curious feature of Proust's parties, a feature that has been under-examined in the critical literature, is that the party itself is very carefully contextualised. Just as important as the party itself and what occurs during the party are its 'before' and its 'after'. Characters

her private interiority is opened out to the external world's values and definitions.

However, this tension between exteriority and interiority, or publicity and private autonomy, was already played out in the opening up of the domestic space, the space of Gertrude and Alice's intimate life, to the public of the expatriate avant-garde at the rue de Fleurus gatherings. What Mark Goble describes as 'opening up a private space to anyone who might stop by [. . .] private life revealed for public view' applies to both *The Autobiography of Alice B. Toklas* and to Gertrude and Alice's home.[9] The domestic is crucial for Stein's writing, not just as the material for her popular *Autobiography* but also as providing the quotidian incidents, locations, personalities and pet-names that generate pieces such as *Tender Buttons* (1914). The personal and domestic – what could be termed, with caution, the autobiographical – are also a central feature of Stein's play-writing and her critical essays.[10] But this does not mean that Stein's writing is confessional; nor does she seek to transfigure the personal and everyday into a revelatory epiphany or intensity.

As Bryony Randall describes, it is possible to identify 'at least three levels of everydayness' in a text such as *Tender Buttons*: 'the everydayness of Stein's choice of object [. . .] the everydayness of her attention to an object' and her textual method as 'examples of everyday meaning-making'.[11] Both Liesl Olson and Randall distinguish Stein's writing as exemplary of a specific strain of modernist engagement with the ordinary and everyday, an engagement with 'ongoing daily time'[12] and 'representation of the ordinary *as* ordinary'.[13] For Olson, Stein demonstrates an investment in 'habit as the essential basis of writing'; and for Randall, Stein's writing typifies the kind of 'distracted attention' that characterises our everyday mode of engagement with the world.[14] So the use of the personal and domestic across Stein's writing – her choice of textual object and the kind of attention that her texts enact and require – can be seen as part of her engagement with the everyday rather than a seeking of publicity for that personal and domestic life. In a similar way, Stein and Toklas's Saturday evening parties at the rue de Fleurus opened up personal space to an external public, but involved domesticating that public and maintaining the everydayness of the parties, rather than creating a spectacular lesbian salon on the lines of Nathalie Barney's rue Jacob gatherings. But when the everyday specialness of Stein's ordinary life becomes special in a monetary way, as it does with the success of *The Autobiography of Alice B. Toklas*, this exposes that ordinary life to the kind of publicity that threatens the sense of linguistic singularity that Stein invests her writing with. Stein wanted to be recognised and read, she enjoyed the money that her bestseller earned, but she also sought to remain faithful to the haecceity of her subject-matter and not translate it into an easy language of communication and exchange. Anxieties about audience and communication, never a problematic issue when Stein invited people into her home, came potentially to contaminate both Stein's attempt to elicit the everyday in her writing and her refusal to fix it in language, a refusal that extended also to her resistance to naming and fixing identity. Stein continued to write of the personal and the everyday, but what she ultimately attempted, in response to the threat of publicity, was to maintain what Goble terms a 'zone of privacy within the language of identity, a way of showing who you are without saying what you are'.[15]

The tension between revelation and publicity, and a linguistic singularity that refuses to conform or typify, underpin Stein's public persona, as epitomised at her rue de Fleurus parties, and characterise her ambivalence about her fame in the 1930s. This ambivalence is textually mapped out in her plays. Drama is fundamentally concerned with disclosure, with presenting and communicating a text to an audience which experiences that text visibly and publicly. Stein's own reservations about drama are articulated in her 1935 lecture 'Plays' and rest substantially on the realisation, which came to her as an adolescent theatre-goer in Oakland and San Francisco, of the asynchronicity between the observer and the action on stage: 'the great difficulty of having my emotion accompany the scene'.[16] Stein characterises her own play-writing, in this essay, in two distinct phases: her early plays, concerned with immediate perception and the continuous present, rejecting 'story' in favour of 'what could be told if one did not tell anything'; and subsequent plays, in which the 'formation' and 'relation' of the play exist 'exactly like a landscape', with no problems of having 'to make acquaintance'.[17]

In both the phases that Stein identifies, her emphasis is on writing plays that express entity over temporality and reject the requirements of explication or identification of character and narrative in favour of being, presence and space. In this, the presence of language in the plays is just as central as the presence of a character or characters, but this is language that is visible, embodied and there, rather than language as an asynchronous experience of hearing. As Stein comments in *Everybody's Autobiography* in relation to listening and seeing, 'my eyes have always told me more than my ears':[18] not a comment on a painterly approach to words but a statement that the unity of the 'complete and actual present'[19] which concerns Stein across her writing can be lost when 'everybody hears too much with their ears and it never makes anything come together'.[20] In 'Plays', Stein highlights the, for her, problematic dichotomy of the theatre, which presents a 'seeing' and a 'hearing' very different from that experienced either in real life or while reading a book. Stein asks, 'is the thing seen or is the thing heard the thing that makes most of its impression upon you at the theatre', and confesses to 'constantly think[ing] about the theatre from the standpoint of sight and sound and its relation to emotion and time'.[21] This suggests that her concern with telling without telling anything and with formation and relation in her plays is at bottom a concern with preventing the discontinuity between experience and perception that occurs when a (performed) text requires the audience-member simultaneously to comprehend diegetic causality and character continuity, while encountering immediate events and language happening before him or her.

Stein's drama is resolutely resistant to the unfolding of plot and acutely aware of the questions she was asking about the revelatory and demonstratory aspects of this genre. For Jane Palatini Bowers, this makes Stein's plays 'adamantly and self-consciously "literary"',[22] and Martin Puchner sees them as evidence of a modernist 'anti-theatrical drama' and, like the rest of Stein's writing, 'based on the high modernist values of engulfment and solitary reading'.[23] As discussed above, although anxious about what an enlarged readership might mean for the linguistic singularity of her writing and its attendant impact on her sense of self, Stein does not enact in her texts the kind of solitary withdrawal that Puchner suggests. Indeed, Stein's writing actively asks for attention: just consider the titles of the plays *A Curtain Raiser* (1913), *Look At Us* (1916), *Listen To Me. A Play* (1936). Her drama in particular is based in a liminal site, similar to the site that the party inhabits, located somewhere between private isolation and the general public, opening up to guests but not leaving the privacy of the personal space. This makes Stein's plays 'closet dramas' in the sense discussed by Nick Salvato in *Uncloseting Drama* rather than in Puchner's definition of the genre. For Salvato, 'closet drama's most fundamental or constant feature is, ironically, its contingency as the mode at the threshold between writing and performance – a threshold that is always, or at least always in danger of, moving'.[24] Closet drama such as Stein's does, therefore, as Salvato points out, straddle the ambiguous verge between the questions about staging and meaning explored in a range of modernist dramas, highlighting the increasing importance of textual materiality in the period. Saint Therese, 'half in and half out of doors' in Stein's *Four Saints in Three Acts* (1927–28),[25] epitomises the position of Stein's drama, poised on the margin between intimacy, the domestic and privacy (of reading), and disclosure, the civic and publicity (of performance). And when Stein writes plays about parties, this margin becomes central to both the form and the theme of her plays.

What Happened: A Play in Five Acts consists of five short acts, as the title proclaims, coming in Act V to 'A regret a single regret makes a door way'.[26] As her first foray into drama, *What Happened* is itself a doorway into the concerns and strategies of Stein's play-writing. Stein relates her coming to drama with *What Happened* in both *The Autobiography of Alice B. Toklas* and in her lecture 'Plays':

> [A]ll of a sudden I began to write Plays [. . .] I had just come home from a pleasant dinner party and I realized then as anybody can know that something is always happening. Something is always happening, anybody knows a quantity of stories of people's lives that are always happening [. . .] So naturally what I wanted to do in my play was what everybody did not always know nor always tell.[27]

In 'Plays', Stein makes it clear that, by eschewing story and exploring instead the continuous present, she was attempting 'to make a play the essence of what happened'.[28] *What Happened* has no identifiable characters or location, and its direct references to the dinner-party that was its inspiration seem to be solely located in the mentions of food ('cake', 'turkey', 'a slice', 'bread') and the dining table ('A wide oak a wide enough oak', 'the perfect central table'). As with the majority of her plays, *What Happened* appears resistant to the conventions of the performable text, but this means it is asking questions of the theatre rather than apotheosising itself as unperformable.[29] Instead of an unfolding temporality and narrative, *What Happened* explores repetitions and increments, most obviously with the comparative and superlative forms of the adjectives 'more' and 'most': 'What is the commonest exchange between more laughing and most' (p. 205). The word 'more' appears fourteen times in various explorations of the being of objects and states, as the play presents the ambient noise – both visual and aural – of a dinner-party; it is concerned with the quotidian rather than the exceptional. Throughout the five acts the play persistently returns to the question of 'what is' and 'is it'; the present indicative verb 'is', appearing eighty times in *What Happened*, encapsulates Stein's textual concern here with identifying the complete and actual present.

In her lecture 'Plays', Stein also demonstrates a concern with the 'excitement' of the theatre that contributes further to the non-coincidence of emotions and the 'nervousness' that results.[30] She contrasts the felt excitement of 'real life' with the exciting scene 'on the stage a thing over which you have no real control':[31] in real life 'there has to be the moment of it all being abreast the emotion, the excitement and the action', whereas in the theatre 'the thing causing your emotion and the excitement in connection with it' are not in step.[32] This means that temporality, discontinuity and 'a relief from excitement' enter into the happening of theatre, which is incompatible with the 'completion of excitement' that is there in 'the real thing'.[33]

Writing a play about a party, a special occasion and the scene of unusual interactions, might seem incompatible with Stein's reflections on the theatre and her determination in her play-writing to present the 'moment of it all' rather than the excitement of event and climax. But *What Happened* explicitly reflects on the nature of the 'occasion', calling on other special occasions – 'Christmas, quite Christmas' (p. 205) and 'A birthday, what is a birthday' (p. 208) – to contrast it with. The excitement here is not the excitement of an extraordinary, climactic event such as a birthday or Christmas; it is the unique but nevertheless everyday stimulation of real life. Stein uses the word 'occasion' four times in *What Happened*, with repetitions emptying the term of its sense of culmination: with these references, she is playing out just that tension between special gathering and trivial small-talk which actually characterises the party. Stein refuses to mark the specialness of the party through the excitement of dramatic narrative structure, multiplying instead the occasions and even modifying the word itself into its adjectival form: 'It is more than one time when the occasion which shows an occasional sharp separation is unanimous' (p. 208). The occasion is 'more than one time'; it is manifold and incidental; it is also an occasion which itself manifests occasional features, such as the sudden breaking of the communal experience of the moment into the 'unanimous' 'separation' into individuals. The occasion for this play is both unique in the celebration of the individual moments that make up the whole of *What Happened*, and completely lacking in the heightened, nervous excitation that Stein deplores in the theatre.

The contrasts that Stein offers to this incidental special occasion are marked by their artificial performance; the birthday party involves specially staged speeches – 'a birthday is a speech' (p. 208) – and the special event of Christmas involves staged photographs:

> A shutter and only shutter and Christmas, quite Christmas, an only shutter and a target a whole color in every center and shooting real shooting and what can hear, that can hear that which makes such an establishment provided with what is provisionary. (p. 205)

The attempt to capture the essence of Christmas, 'quite Christmas', in a photograph is represented as a violent closure, with the repetition and half rhyme of 'shutter' and 'shooting'. The 'only shutter' is deterministic and solitary, and the 'real shooting' is both an actual threat and a killing of the real as it is trapped in the static image. This seen image is contrasted with the heard, which, here, is connected with 'what is provisionary' rather than fixed. This is not, of course, evidence for a general resistance in Stein's writing, or life, to photography: it is simply that, within *What Happened*, the Christmas photograph figures forth a staged, fixed moment of excitement, in contrast to the continuous, vibrant present of the party-play.

Photography features again in the final act, connected here to the 'door way' which itself suggests the ambivalent position of the play, poised between text and stage:

> A regret a single regret makes a door way. What is a door way, a door way is a photograph.
> What is a photograph a photograph is a sight and a sight is always a sight of something. Very likely there is a photograph that gives color if there is then there is that color that does not change any more than it did when there was much more use for photography. (p. 209)

For Ulla Dydo, this is a reasonably straightforward evocation of the conclusion of the party:

> at the end, after a photograph of the party, we move with regrets into the doorway that narrows the view to departure. We leave with a picture of what happened framed in the mind. Long before color photography, it is a permanent, vivid image filled with the color that fills the play.[34]

But ambivalence about the fixity of the photograph persists here in the 'regret', the 'color that does not change' and the past tense 'was' of the final clause. The leave-taking is a narrowing, as Dydo suggests, but its transformation into a permanent photograph is in stark contrast to the vivid noise of the party. Crucially, the photograph is 'always a sight of something', an identified fixed object or thing emptied of its potential entity. The frame of the 'door way' which could offer possibility, which could be that liminal space of action, is converted into the enclosed border of the photograph and the static proscenium of the stage, dividing the staged (photograph/play) from the real.

A more resonant conclusion to *What Happened* is offered at the close of the preceding act, where Stein essays what will become a characteristic refusal in her drama to accept the conventions of form; in *What Happened* there is a finishing before the supposedly conclusive fifth act. Act IV ends:

> . . . one hat in a curtain that is rising higher, one landing and many many more, and many more many more many many more. (p. 209)

Instead of the wooden proscenium or frame, here we have the fabric curtain and it is 'rising', not separating staged from real, but offering a stage or 'landing' that is a place of arrival and also the act of arrival. The 'landing' is, moreover, multiplied incrementally and infinitely, opening out *What Happened* into the boundless possibilities of ordinary occurrence. In this play, therefore, both the theatrical 'event' and the party are subsumed into Stein's iteration of the everyday.

A Play Called Not And Now is immediately striking, not for the ordinary possibilities it poses, but for the manifold recurrences of the verb 'to look', most often in variations of the phrases 'look like'/'looked like' and 'look at'/'looked at'. The extremes of repetition in this play lead Richard Bridgeman to conclude that 'the play as a whole is very dull',[35] but Stein's emphasis on looking and looking like are key to *Not And Now*'s presentation of a celebrity-filled Hollywood party.[36] Structurally, the play comprises four acts, including two Act IIIs,[37] and it begins with an opening section that lists five Characters, six Women and a further figure, 'Doctor Gidon':

Characters
A man who looks like Dashiell Hammett
A man who looks like Picasso
A man who looks like Charlie Chaplin
A man who looks like Lord Berners
A man who looks like David Green.
Women
A woman who looks like Anita Loos
A woman who looks like Gertrude Atherton
A woman who looks like Lady Diana Grey
A woman who looks like Katherine Cornell
A woman who looks like Daisy Fellowes
A woman who looks like Mrs. Andrew Greene
    These are the characters and this is what they do.
    A man who looks like Doctor Gidon and some one who looks like each one of the other characters.
The play will now begin.
The difference between not and now. That is what makes any one look like some one. All the characters are there and the one that looks like Doctor Gidon is the one that says what has just been said only it is not what Doctor Gidon would say but is said by the one that is like him.
The characters are now all in order.
They move and speak.[38]

This opening section blends what might be didascalia, paratext and dialogue (is it Doctor Gidon who 'says what has just been said', that is, the two sentences preceding this statement?), with an ironic character list that opens up a gap between appearance and self, or between 'public self (character)' and 'private self (real person)' for Jane Bowers, or between 'projected self' or 'identity' and 'self hidden from view' or 'entity' for Julia Fawcett.[39] The figures in the play are always referred to as 'the one who looked like . . .', the past participle taking over from the present tense 'looks' near the beginning of the first act. This means that at every instance of a figure's mention we are reminded of the visibility of that figure and our own act, as reader/audience, of looking at them.[40]

Not And Now offers a very different presentation of a party in comparison to *What Happened*: with so much of the text reporting on the 'Characters' and 'Women', it is peopled in a way the earlier play about a party simply is not. For many critics the celebrity names are key to understanding *Not And Now*: Bowers argues that the play dramatises the fact that a celebrity or public self 'is not a real self',[41] and Salvato sees the play's 'obsessive theme' as 'self-alienation'.[42] There is indeed a clear sense that *Not And Now* investigates the functioning of celebrity culture and its dislocation of individual identity and, given the Hollywood setting of the party, interrogates the role of the gaze in constructing celebrity-as-commodity. But the play is not a wholly negative response to either fame or the theatre and the complex delegation of character identity is not a refusal of public identity. *Not And Now* plays with the obvious (in a theatrical production) fact that there are people playing characters in a play, attempting to be 'like' these characters in their performance before an audience, rather than actually being these characters. But Stein confounds even this easy meaning for the 'ones who look like' in *Not And Now*, explaining that 'The one who was like the one who was like Charlie Chaplin that would make two and there was only one came in as he came in that is he was all alone as he came in' (p. 428). If 'the one who looked like Charlie Chaplin' in this play is 'one' (a word repeated 473 times in *Not And Now*) then we do not have identities multiplied by performativity. Rather, we have 'one' constructed by the act of looking and, implicitly, liking.

Not And Now has some direct dialogue (though not necessarily marked as such) alongside reported speech, and the play consists of this speech and of descriptions of the movements and interactions of the figures. However, though there is detail on the interaction there is often little detail of what is spoken:

> The one that looked like Anita Loos did not say anything the one that looked like Dashiell Hammett did not say anything to her. The one that looked like Gertrude Atherton said something, the one that looked like Picasso did not say anything to her. The one that looked like Lady Diane Grey said a great deal. (p. 425)

Thus, while there are instances of direct speech in *Not And Now*, the greater part of the play is reported speech and description and this forces the attention onto 'looking', both the looking repeated within the text and the looking which is what the text mostly consists of. Instead of a disjunction of hearing and seeing, producing asynchronicity and nervousness, the emphasis is on seeing, but in a way which forces the audience/reader of *Not And Now* to an acute consciousness of her/his own actions of looking in the process of meaning-making, whether this is the act of looking at words, looking at actors on stage or looking at the glamorous celebrities of popular culture (Hollywood stars, popular writers, eccentric peers, avant-garde icons). Moreover, as Fawcett points out, the play highlights the 'unarticulated subject of "to look"' and 'Stein refuses to clarify whether the unmarked looker implied in her insistent verb watches the events and narrates the play as a character on stage [. . .] as a director or playwright [. . .] or as an audience member'.[43] Acknowledging, as Fawcett does, that Stein's writing in *Not And Now* causes the subject to disappear even as her/his presence is grammatically invoked makes it clear how Stein maintains her/a privacy in this public text about an intimately public event: it is her way of showing without saying and fixing.

Stein's privacy was breached, as she saw it, in the 1930s by the money her audience was willing to pay. *Not And Now*, as part of its exploration of celebrity, publicity and identity as these feature at a party full of famous people, considers money in detail. The majority of Act III_1 scene iv is a disquisition on money, a topic that is introduced in the first act with the reflection that 'They knew that money was a bother' (p. 426). Whereas this first mention of money is followed by various figures looking to see if, or looking like, they have money, III_1, iv presents declarative statements on money itself, attributed to 'the one who is like Dr. Gidon':

> The only difference between man and monkey
> Is what money makes.
> If there is no money then like anything
> They eat what they have.
> But money is not so.
> It is kept
> That is what it is.
> And nothing is kept except what money is. (p. 432)

There are close parallels here with statements Stein makes in *Everybody's Autobiography* that money is 'really the difference between men and animals [. . .] money is purely a human conception' (p. 28), but in *Not*

And Now this idea is made concrete through the verbal play where 'money' and the 'k' of 'makes' is literally the difference between the words 'man' and 'monkey'. Emphasised here, with the repetition of 'k', is the keeping of money, its accumulation, the human abstraction of money as a mode of exchange into money as an essence or 'what it is'.

The essence of money as 'purely a human conception' is exemplified in further instances of verbal play in this scene in the sequence involving what 'the one who is like Picasso' 'is to do when he see money': 'Hold it and hoe it', 'Money can not go and say so' (p. 432). The horticultural references 'hoe' and 'so[w]', which gesture towards fertile abundance and the natural world, are contrasted with the ideas of stasis and dry accumulation expressed by 'hold' and 'not go'. Money cannot move or express itself; it has no becoming:

> There is no no in seen.
> There is no in money.
> There is so in seen.
> There is no so in money. (p. 433)

The seen/scene, the action of looking/the action of the play, does not involve a denial ('no') but it remains open to possibilities ('so'). The problem arises when that looking/text becomes a financial transaction, when the 'no' substitutes for the 'so'. Nevertheless, Stein emphasises the inevitability of money in human society in *Everybody's Autobiography*: 'after all money is money if you live together and as the world is now all covered over everybody has to live together and if you live together call it what you like it has to be money, and that is the way it is',[44] or, as she puts it more playfully in *Not And Now*, 'without money there is no butter' (p. 432). The problem arises, as Stein shows in *Everybody's Autobiography*, when money completely erases and replaces identity. This is the case when 'The one who looks like Charlie Chaplin arranges neatly that he is not there. Where is he. He is not there. And where is money. Money is there' (p. 432). *Not And Now* is necessarily aware of money and fame in its account of the Hollywood party, but these are only problematic concepts when they converge to replace identity with a celebrity-commodity.

For both Salvato and Fawcett, the key to understanding *Not And Now* lies in one of the celebrities who wasn't actually at the Hollywood party. Lord Berners, listed as one of the 'Characters' of *Not And Now*, was a friend of Stein but was not in attendance and Salvato sees the inclusion of this openly gay man as the 'solution to the riddle' of *Not And Now*, reading 'the mysterious assemblage of women' in Act III$_1$ as 'really an assemblage of queer men' and part of the play's 'implicit valuation

[. . .] of a queer sensibility'.[45] Picasso was not at the party either and Fawcett takes this 'Character' as a reference instead to 'a Picasso', that is, Picasso's famous 1905–6 portrait of Stein, leading her to conclude that the 'one who looked like [a] Picasso' figures as a form of 'appropriation of Stein's identity' that is interrogated in the play.[46] But it is just as easy to use some celebrities who were actually at the party – the famous popular writers Anita Loos and Dashiell Hammett – as the catalyst for a reading of the play. Both Loos and Hammett had had their most successful novels adapted for cinema (*Gentlemen Prefer Blondes* in 1928 and *The Thin Man* in 1934, respectively) and their presence in *Not And Now* could signal an anxiety, not about celebrity or success, but about representation and translation into popular media forms.

Hammett's presence is particularly resonant: Stein specifically requested that Hammett be invited to the party, as she relates on the opening pages of *Everybody's Autobiography*, and her mention of Hammett there triggers Stein to reflect that 'It is very nice being a celebrity a real celebrity who can decide who they want to meet and say so and they come or do not come as you want them.'[47] Her enjoyment of detective fiction is well documented and it was the genre she adopted to write herself out of her block after the publication of *The Autobiography of Alice B. Toklas*. Stein's interest in detective fiction, which she described as 'the only real modern novel form', lay in the fact that it 'gets rid of human nature by having the man dead to be begin with the hero is dead to begin with and so you have so to speak got rid of the event before the book begins'.[48] Hammett's *The Thin Man* (1934) epitomises this completely as the 'Thin Man' of the title, who turns out to have been the murder victim, is present in the novel only in the representations (forged letters and telegrams, false sightings, faked encounters) that various other characters fabricate. The absolute absence of the eponymous hero, whose body has been reduced to a skeleton, and the epistemological uncertainty of the detective Nick Charles's solution to the mystery – the final phrase of the novel is 'but it's all pretty unsatisfactory' – have significant consequences for *Not And Now*. The play is Stein's own way of getting rid of the event, refusing plot, climax and celebrity heroes in her play about a party, to allow her writing to turn a distracted attention instead to the incremental and quotidian. What Salvato registers as a critique of the 'triviality and tedium of party conversation'[49] is actually the fully realised and celebrated essence of what Stein intends with *Not And Now*.

Not And Now ends with the statement 'that was what was happening', an interesting verbal echo of Stein's first play, but for Bowers this directly indicates the failure Stein is acknowledging with her play, that the 'not and now [...] cannot be merged' and so '[t]he written play is a record of what is "not", no matter how closely it registered the "now" of its composition'.[50] But Stein's use of the past progressive actually suggests a continuity, indicating that something was going on, something persisted; it is a deliberate denial of climax and an articulation of the quotidian. *Not And Now* is not exciting: 'it might have been exciting' (p. 424) we are told, but it deliberately is not. The play inhabits the ongoing ordinariness of the party, rather than glamorising its celebrity guests and their conversation; 'what did they say. They said everything' (p. 427). What is fundamental here is the rejection of a plot or anything that would seek to transform the ordinariness of being into artificial excitement. We are instead simply in the 'middle': 'in the middle of looking like him he went on looking like him that is what the one did who looked like him' (p. 434). It is not just this 'one' who 'went on looking like': we are told that the Characters and Women look like themselves 'one Sunday morning', 'one Sunday', 'every Sunday', 'Sunday morning afternoon and evening', 'and every week day' (p. 434). This moment, the party, is no different, not because there is no difference, but because every moment, every day, is singular, just as every person is unique in his or her own ordinary sameness: 'there is one and he looks like each one not the same each one but each one as is the one which is that one' (p. 438). The 473 instances of the word 'one' in the play are, every one, singular expressions of singularity. What *Not And Now* presents is a Hollywood party that, extraordinarily enough, epitomises the exceptional essence of everyday being.

Stein's dramatic writing in *What Happened*, *Not And Now* and elsewhere fundamentally reveals how 'something is always happening', making everything special and not singling out an exceptional moment or entity. *What Happened* refuses to stage the party/play as an occasion and replaces the climax of the theatre event with an incremental exploration of the quotidian. The play is notable particularly for its lack of the obvious markers of a dramatic text – characters, speeches, stage directions – but its orientation, as displayed in the full title *What Happened: A Play*, is towards the public space of the theatre. *Not And Now* shows a marked alteration in Stein's play-writing, responding not least to the change in her status as a writer. Now that she is herself a celebrity, her play is acutely conscious of its own potential visibility, enacted through the central concern with highly visible characters. The Hollywood party of *Not And Now* is much more readily a spectacular event and so, perhaps more adamantly than Stein's first play, it insists on the commonplace and refuses to stabilise the nature of public identity. Grammatically creating a zone of privacy, where the 'real' speaker of the text and the 'essential' identity of the celebrities can persist, the play presents a showing that does not dictate but resolutely inhabits the uncertain, liminal space that Stein's drama delineates. In *What Happened* and *Not And Now* the forum of the party embodies an ambiguous combination of intimacy and publicity, privacy and display, which directly mirrors the 'closet' status of Stein's drama and is also fundamental to her more accessible, popular 'autobiographical' writing.

Notes

1. Sarah Bay-Cheng, *Mama Dada: Gertrude Stein's Avant-Garde Theater* (New York: Routledge, 2005), p. 35.
2. Stein's only publications to this date had been *Three Lives*, published, at her own expense, in New York by the Grafton Press in 1909, and 'A Portrait of Mabel Dodge at the Villa Curonia', privately printed by Dodge in Florence in 1912. Gibb had taken a couple of copies of 'A Portrait of Mabel Dodge at the Villa Curonia' with him to Dublin during a show of his pictures and 'it was then that the Dublin writers in the cafés heard Gertrude Stein read aloud. Doctor Gogarty, Harry Gibb's host and admirer, loved to read it aloud himself and have others read it aloud'. Gertrude Stein, *The Autobiography of Alice B. Toklas* (1933) (London: Penguin, 1966), p. 128.
3. Steven Watson, *Prepare for Saints: Gertrude Stein, Virgil Thomson, and the Mainstreaming of American Modernism* (Berkeley: University of California Press, 2000), pp. 4–5; see this study for a full account of the development and staging of *Four Saints in Three Acts* in America in 1934.
4. Bay-Cheng, *Mama Dada*, p. 35.
5. Stein, *The Autobiography of Alice B. Toklas*, pp. 10–11.
6. Gertrude Stein, *The Making of Americans* (1925) (Normal: Dalkey Archive Press, 1995), pp. 292, 289.
7. Gertrude Stein, *Everybody's Autobiography* (1936) (London: Virago, 1985), pp. 27, 32.
8. Ibid., p. 34.
9. Mark Goble, *Beautiful Circuits: Modernism and the Mediated Life* (New York: Columbia University Press, 2010) p. 99.
10. Marc Robinson notes how 'Stein's love of company, the comings and goings at Fleurus, and even the travails of life with Alice work their way into the plays'. Marc Robinson, *The Other American Drama* (Baltimore: Johns Hopkins University Press, 1997), p. 20. Martin Puchner comments on 'Stein's characteristic combination of autobiography and theory' in her essay writing. Martin Puchner, *Stage Fright: Modernism, Anti-Theatricality, and Drama* (Baltimore: Johns Hopkins University Press, 2002), p. 102.
11. Bryony Randall, *Modernism, Daily Time and Everyday Life* (Cambridge: Cambridge University Press, 2007), p. 118.
12. Ibid., p. 7.
13. Liesl Olson, *Modernism and the Ordinary* (New York: Oxford University Press, 2009), p. 5.
14. Ibid., p. 97; Randall, *Modernism, Daily Time*, p. 121.

15. Goble, *Beautiful Circuits*, p. 144.

16. Stein, 'Plays' (1935), in *Lectures in America* (New York: Random House, 1935), pp. 93–131: p. 114.

17. Ibid., pp. 119, 125, 122.

18. Stein, *Everybody's Autobiography*, p. 69.

19. Stein, 'Plays', p. 105.

20. Stein, *Everybody's Autobiography*, p. 69.

21. Stein, 'Plays', pp. 103, 104.

22. Jane Palatini Bowers, *'They Watch Me as They Watch This': Gertrude Stein's Metadrama* (Philadelphia: University of Pennsylvania Press, 1991), p. 2.

23. Puchner, *Stage Fright*, pp. 105, 103.

24. Nick Salvato, *Uncloseting Drama: American Modernism and Queer Performance* (New Haven: Yale University Press, 2010), p. 5.

25. Gertrude Stein, *Four Saints in Three Acts*, in *Last Operas and Plays* (New York: Rhinehart: 1949), p. 445.

26. Stein, *What Happened: A Play in Five Acts* (1913), in *Geography and Plays* (Mineola: Dover Publications, 1999), pp. 205–9: p. 209; subsequent page references are given in the text.

27. Stein 'Plays', pp. 118–19.

28. Stein 'Plays', p. 119. 'It was during that winter that Gertrude Stein began to write plays. They began with one entitled, It Happened a Play. This was written about a dinner party given by Harry and Bridget Gibb'. Stein, *The Autobiography of Alice B. Toklas*, p. 145.

29. For details of professional performances of *What Happened*, see Bay-Cheng, *Mama Dada*, Appendix B.

30. Stein, 'Plays', p. 95.

31. Ibid., p. 98.

32. Ibid., pp. 100, 101.

33. Ibid., p. 96.

34. Ulla E. Dydo, *A Stein Reader* (Evanston: Northwestern University Press, 1993), pp. 268–9.

35. Richard Bridgeman, *Gertrude Stein in Pieces* (New York: Oxford University Press, 1970), p. 285.

36. The party is described by Toklas in her memoir: 'Conversation at dinner was fairly lively. Mr Chaplin had brought with him Paulette Goddard, who was an enfant terrible. There was also a Spanish diplomat and our hostess' brother, who was a film director. After dinner there were some guests who came, amongst them Anita Loos, to whom I took an immediate fancy. The film directors gathered around Miss Stein and said, We would like to know how you came to have your enormous popularity, and she said, By having a small audience, whereupon they shoved their chairs away from her, discouraged with what she had to advise.' Alice B. Toklas, *What Is Remembered* (1963) (London: Abacus, 1989), p. 152.

37. When these two Act IIIs are referred to here, they will be distinguished as Act III$_1$ (the first Act III) and Act III$_2$ (the second Act III).

38. Gertrude Stein, *A Play Called Not And Now* (1936), in *Last Operas and Plays*, pp. 422–39: p. 422. Hereafter page numbers are given in the text.

39. Bowers, *'They Watch Me'*, p. 88; Julia Fawcett, 'Looking For The One

Who Looks Like Someone: The Unmarked Subject(s) in Gertrude Stein's *A Play Called Not and Now*', *Modern Drama* 53:2 (2010), pp. 137–58: p. 142.

40. Although *Not And Now* foregrounds the 'looking' of an audience, the only professional production of this play has been as a puppet play at the Heston International Festival of Puppet Theater in New York in 1994; see Bay-Cheng, *Mama Dada*, p. 162.
41. Bowers, '*They Watch Me*', p. 88.
42. Salvato, *Uncloseting Drama*, pp. 116, 118.
43. Fawcett, 'Looking For The One Who Looks Like Someone', pp. 145, 152.
44. Stein, *Everybody's Autobiography*, p. 269.
45. Salvato, *Uncloseting Drama*, p. 122.
46. Fawcett, 'Looking For The One Who Looks Like Someone', p. 148.
47. Stein, *Everybody's Autobiography,* p. xxi.
48. Gertrude Stein, 'What Are Masterpieces and Why Are There So Few of Them', in Patricia Meyerowitz (ed.), *Gertrude Stein: Look at Me Now and Here I Am: Writings and Lectures 1911–1945* (London: Peter Owen, 2004), p. 149.
49. Salvato, *Uncloseting Drama*, p. 117.
50. Bowers, '*They Watch Me*', p. 90.

Chapter 9

The Interracial Party of Modernist Primitivism and the Black 'After-Party'

Margo Natalie Crawford

At these times, the Negro drags his captors captive. On occasions, I have been amazed and amused watching white people dancing to a Negro band in a Harlem cabaret; attempting to throw off the crusts and layers of inhibitions laid on by sophisticated civilization; striving to yield to the feel and experience of abandon; seeking to recapture a taste of primitive joy in life and living; trying to work their way back into that jungle which was the original Garden of Eden; in a word, doing their best to pass for colored. (James Weldon Johnson, *Along This Way*)[1]

She wasn't, she told herself, a jungle creature. She cloaked herself in a faint disgust as she watched the entertainers throw themselves about to the bursts of syncopated jangle, and when the time came again for the patrons to dance, she declined. (Nella Larsen, *Quicksand*)[2]

The Harlem Renaissance of the 1920s and 1930s, in some of the 1960s and 1970s Black Arts Movement critiques, was an artistic movement of African Americans frolicking with the oppressors. Whereas the salons and sociability of Gertrude Stein, Muriel Draper and other modernists have been celebrated as the gathering of kindred spirits, the Black Arts Movement's assessments of the Harlem Renaissance set it up as an interracial party or spectacle of assimilation, in which the self-determination of the Negro was constantly jeopardised. Black Arts Movement writers critiqued the role of white patrons in the Harlem Renaissance and an alleged desire, on the part of the African American writers, to assimilate into a dominant (white) aesthetic. Amiri Baraka, in 'The Myth of a "Negro Literature"' (1963), for example, argues that the majority of Harlem Renaissance literature remained mediocre art, due to the imitation of white 'high art'.[3]

In studies of the Harlem Renaissance, the iconic party is the 1920s or 1930s rent-party: the house-parties, with small fees for entry, that enabled tenants to pay rent. A focus on a wider modernist party dynamic, however, deepens the key inquiries that have shaped Harlem Renaissance scholarship. Our understanding of the cultural appropriations, the performances of race and the complexity of modernist primitivism expands when we focus on the literal and symbolic interracial party dynamic of the Harlem Renaissance. But the complexity of this larger party dynamic is embedded in some of the depictions of the rent-party. Wallace Thurman describes the rent-party of the Harlem Renaissance as a 'commercialization of spontaneous pleasure in order to pay the landlord' and 'a joyful intimate party, open to the public yet held in a private home'.[4] This language signals that the phenomenon of people hosting parties (with strangers and family and friends) in their homes produced a certain intertwining of the public and private. People gained access to other people's private space and experienced it as public space. Thurman's emphasis on the joyful nature of entering into other people's privacy and making one's private space public is very different from the depiction, in one of his unpublished essays, of the sadness that suffused the rent-party. Thurman writes, '[d]espite the freedom and frenzy of these parties they are seldom joyous affairs. On the contrary they are rather sad and depressing. A tragic undercurrent runs through the music and is reflected in the eyes and faces of the dancers' (pp. 73–4). The notion of an 'undercurrent' of a party can be extended into a way of thinking about the undercurrents of the Harlem Renaissance. Just as the music and dance of jazz and blues had this note of melancholy underneath the 'frenzy', the literature of the movement contains this sense of a party that has stopped being pleasurable.

The final scene of Nella Larsen's *Passing* (1929) epitomises this sense of the end of the party. Clare, the now iconic figure, in African American literature, of passing for white, dies. John Bellew, the white person who intrudes on this party and confronts his wife with his knowledge that she has been passing for white, is the same person who, in an earlier scene in the novel, revels in his wife's amazingly seductive ability to darken, during the summer, to the extent that she almost looks like a Negro. He uses the term 'nigger' (not 'Negro') and fully performs antiblack racism as he conveys his affection for his wife, whom he believes is a white woman who gets an unusually dark tan during the summer. Bellew approaches the gaze of classic racialised modernist primitivism when he enjoys seeing 'white' as dark but still 'white'. The darkness that seduced the modernist primitivists who elevated the raw as the highest value was a darkness that was most appealing when it was collected, rearranged and interpreted through the white modernist lens. I will argue that, when primitivism became white modernists' playful experiment with escaping white privilege, it gained a performative space that had the shape of an interracial party, hosted by white people, who invite black people to join in the fun.

The complexity of performances of modernist primitivism surfaces when the interracial party of primitivism is compared with the images of the black party within the larger party of primitivism. Larsen's image of the party in *Quicksand* is one of the most telling depictions of African American responses to racialised primitivism. After the dinner-party in Chapter 11, there is an 'after-party', with riotous dancing. This party is a core example of the black parties in which black people process the modernist primitivism that has been projected onto black bodies. Helga initially dances with pure joy as she feels that the 'essence of life seemed bodily motion'. Once the music ends, she regrets the dance and tells herself that she is not a 'jungle creature'. [5] Larsen captures the everyday dance through the racial primitivist trap that equated the 'jungle' and black bodies. Helga cannot seize the aesthetic of 'bodily motion' without feeling stuck in a demeaning racial position.

In the 'jungle creature' party scene in *Quicksand*, the release that dance produces is the release produced when a group of black people dance without the presence of a white gaze. Nonetheless, when the music ends, Helga feels the power of the gaze that conflates black people dancing with 'jungle creatures'. Larsen depicts non-self-conscious dance as a higher state of consciousness that allows the black dancer not to think about the antiblack racism that makes the 'jungle creature' such a demeaning position. The role of dance in African American entanglements with primitivism is illuminating. The powerful, beautiful and tormented dances in the modernist primitivist party are ways in which people animated a discourse that was written on their bodies.

Langston Hughes's short story 'Rejuvenation Through Joy' (1933) sheds light on black modernist dancers' nitty-gritty wrestling with the straitjacket that primitivism could have become. Lesche, who is pretending to be a knowledgeable spiritualist in order to get his wealthy white women clients to pay for sessions at his 'colony', is revealed, at the very end of the story, as possibly being a black man passing for white. Lesche makes dance a key feature of his 'rejuvenation' classes. As he teaches his white women clients that they must discover their 'life-center, the balancing point', he advises, 'Look at the Negroes. They know how to move from the feet up, from the head down. Their centers live.'[6] But when Lesche guides the rehearsal for one of the performative classes, the black woman dancer, Tulane Lucas, is depicted as 'gliding', not gyrating in the manner that we might expect when we hear the idea of the centre that 'lives'. The gliding is depicted in the following manner: 'The jazz band began to cry *Mood Indigo* in the best manner of the immortal Duke Ellington. Lesche began to speak in his great soft voice. Bushy-haired Tulane Lucas began to glide across the floor' (p. 87). Gliding is a delightful way of rethinking the black modernist dancers' navigation of the potential straitjacket of primitivism. Hughes, in this same short story, offers images of bowing as yet another way of visualising the erotic, primitivised centre as a gesture, not a racial essence. The images of Lesche's bowing are a stunning interpretation of the black modernists' after-party, as the bending of the body that is supposed to shake and wiggle into a hard, frozen, mechanical reproduction of *grace*. Hughes writes:

> 'They (the Negroes) walk, they stand, they dance to their drum beats, their earth rhythms. They squat, they kneel, they lie – but they never, in their natural states, never sit in chairs. They do not mood and brood. No! They live through motion, through movement, through music, through joy! (Remember my lecture, 'Negroes and Joy'?) Ladies, and gentlemen, I offer you today – rejuvenation through joy.'
>   Lesche bowed and bowed as he left the platform. With *the greatest of grace* he returned to bow again to applause, that was thunderous. To a ballroom that was full of well-dressed women and cultured men, he bowed and bowed. (p. 72, emphasis added)

Some bows can make the person being honoured seem submissive. Hughes shows that the grace dancers express is different from the 'jungle dance' that worries Helga. We can rethink the dance of modernist primitivism as the difficult space where a certain grace was achieved, in the black after-party, by African American modernists who did not fully internalise the jungle creature ideology. Countering an external gaze that imagined a jungle while watching black bodies dancing, black modernists may have gained a renewed sense of the difference between jungle movements and controlled movements. The sense of control is what is lost when white subjects perform a stereotype of black dance. In the film *The Jerk* (1979), as Steve Martin's character searches for the beat (saying, 'I can feel it. I can feel it'), the jerkiness of his movements dramatises the difference between rhythm and flow and the uncontrolled wildness that looks like a jolt.

The angles and bending that shaped the black after-party of primitivism look even more pronounced when Hughes's depiction of the repeated bow is compared to the angles and bends in the art of Aaron Douglas. Years after the Harlem Renaissance, Douglas explained that he deliberately decided, after his initial reluctance, to do 'this primitive thing'.[7] Douglas decided that primitivism was not necessarily a trap that made black artists produce 'naïve' art for a patronising audience. In a letter to Langston Hughes, Douglas writes:

Plunge [. . .] into the very depths of the soul of our people, and drag forth material, crude, rough, neglected. Then let's sing it, dance it, write it, paint it. Let's do the impossible. Let's create something transcendentally material, mystically objective. Earthy. Spiritually earthy. Dynamic.[8]

The bending of figures in his semi-abstract woodcuts shows that doing 'the impossible' was the controlled movement in the midst of the full plunging. Douglas, in his images of the black dance-party, makes room for the African American enjoyment of the primitive plunge. The controlled movement of this pleasurable plunge into primitivism can be seen in the lines in Douglas's woodcuts. When Douglas evokes the minstrel images, he sometimes places the full lips and other signs of black-face minstrelsy in the context of a dance-party. These are the images that open up my argument about the party, the pleasure and the fantasy of white primitivism. Racialised primitivism may indeed, as Anne Cheng argues in *Second Skin: Josephine Baker and the Modern Surface* (2011), make Picasso and others experience a certain 'shattering', but it also produces a type of entertainment and comfort that is often rewritten as self-alienation and traumatic dislocation.[9] Cheng's sense that Picasso was surely appropriating the African masks as objects but also 'shattered' by them does not make room for the power tied to the type of shattering that allows the white primitivist to be possessed by the other in a manner that makes *being possessed by* coterminous with *collecting that which possesses you.*

The tone of a party changes when there is a collection process happening that makes white uncontrolled self-abandon, for some white party-goers, also a state of a certain type of control of the other. But many Harlem Renaissance texts show that African Americans used images of controlled abandon as a way of thinking about an aesthetic that was set apart from whiteness. Elmer A. Carter, for example, in his analysis of Billy Pierce's tap-dancing across the colour-line and his teaching others to tap-dance, writes:

The stamp of the Billy Pierce studio is unmistakably imprinted on every one of his pupils. He gives them something other teachers cannot give. It is something of Negro abandon, enhanced and yet partially concealed by exquisite grace and a perfect sense of rhythm.[10]

'Negro abandon' is depicted in Carter's essay as a staccato 'tap tap tap tap'. The acoustics of Negro abandon (sounds such as Carter's depiction of the staccato beat) are not the same as the visual images that continue to make the 'jungle creature' the centre of analyses of the role of blackness in white modernist primitivism. The sound of controlled abandon may be the sound of black chant. Scholars such as Aldon Lynn Nielsen have identified the role of chant in black postmodern poetics. Chant has a primitive aura.[11] Consider Lafcadio Hearn's depiction of chant in the 1878 text *Two Years in the French West Indies*: 'His chant is cavernous, abysmal – booms from his chest like the sound of a drum beaten in the bottom of a well [. . .] and all chant after him, in a chanting like the rushing of many waters, and with triple clapping of hands.'[12] Chant's seeming primitiveness is its ability, through repetition of the same sounds, to create an inner space, like a 'bottom of a well', that is an altered state of consciousness (a state of trance) and controlled abandon. In the midst of the modernist primitivist party, this inner space of controlled abandon may have been achieved by many involuntary black party-goers.

In *Cane* (1923), Jean Toomer uses chant and trance to call for an understanding of African American controlled abandon as beautiful, not degrading. The final story in *Cane*, 'Kabnis', ends with an underground party (a party in a basement) that is haunted by the presence of Father John, the elderly man whose controlled abandon and primitiveness greatly frustrate the young Kabnis. Kabnis parties and moves with wild abandon while Father John actually embodies that other state of abandonment – the state of being left behind. After Kabnis's drunken stupor and sexual abandon, he cannot bear to see the bust-like, immobile nature of Father John and he cannot bear Father John's blindness and initial muteness. When Father John speaks, he begins to talk about sin and the 'white folks' who made the Bible lie. Kabnis simply wants to continue partying; he does not want to hear this heavy reminder, presumably from a man who was actually formerly enslaved, about the larger current and historical context of the modernist party. Father John speaks as if he is in a state of trance (or the shock tied to post-slavery trauma). Toomer ends *Cane* with this tension between Kabnis's desire for the 'new and up to date' and Father John's embodiment of the old. The circular nature of *Cane*, the final image of the sun rising, makes the tension of Kabnis's uncontrolled abandon and Father John's controlled abandon connect to the opening section's use of a chant about the sun setting and the need to see the ephemeral and evanescent before it disappears. Toomer makes chant's production of inner space ('O cant you see it, O cant you see it / Her skin is like dusk on the eastern horizon / [. . .] When the sun goes down') pivot on skin's interiority.[13] Cheng argues that modernism often plays with the inner and outer dimensions of skin. Kabnis, unlike the dark-skinned Father John, is 'lemon colored'. Throughout *Cane*, Toomer makes light skin a sign of becoming and evanescence, whereas the dark skin of characters such as King Barlo and

Father John is tied to rootedness. The final conflict, in the underground party, is the conflict between the aesthetic of becoming and uncontrolled abandon and the aesthetic of righteous rootedness and controlled abandon. This tension between becoming and rootedness is embedded in black responses to modernist primitivism. Instead of *being* the primitive, how did black subjects gain access to the freedom of *becoming* the primitive, the freedom of liminality that made primitivism consciously or unconsciously enjoyable for white subjects? On the other hand, how did African Americans claim their right to be a spectator of the primitivist party (not an entertainer within it)?

Watching the show (not always being in the show) generated the poetics of black modernist controlled abandon. Consider Claude McKay's poem 'Negro Dancers' (1925). The speaker states, ''Tis best to sit and gaze; my heart then dances / To the lithe bodies gliding slowly by.'[14] This sonnet is in full conversation with Helene Johnson's 'Sonnet to a Negro in Harlem' (1927). Johnson violates the rules of rhyme of the sonnet form as she connects the modernist play with the sonnet to the play with the typical primitivist relation between the patronising spectator and the humble object of study. The most pronounced image of primitivism in the poem is: 'Your head thrown back in rich, barbaric song, / Palm trees and mangoes stretched before your eyes.' The pronounced defiance of the primitivist script is the woman's 'arrogant' laughter and 'supercilious feet': 'Why urge ahead your supercilious feet? / [. . .] 'I love your laughter arrogant and bold'.[15] Once the primitive attitude gains this haughty texture, the overall feel of the party changes, and the overall texture of black modernist literature changes. The 'feet' in the sonnet (the meter itself) gain a 'supercilious' edge; Harlem Renaissance writers begin to experiment with new forms, new ways of expressing the grace of controlled movement and the delight of abandon. Zora Neale Hurston, undoubtedly, epitomises the haughty African American approach to primitivism. Her famous words 'No, I do not weep at the world – I am too busy sharpening my oyster knife' and the iconic photographs of her with the haughty hat twisted to the side are as telling as her deep interest in recording and aestheticising the folk and the primitive.[16]

In the play *Mr. Frog* (1930), Hurston uses an Aristophanic 'frog chorus' as she depicts a wedding-party set in the time 'when animals talked'. This wedding-party is as primitive as animals are in the human imagination and as refined and sophisticated as the modern dance is at the beginning of the play. The temporal and spatial dimensions of modernist primitivism could be described in the way that Hurston describes this opening dance – a 'violent wind dance'.[17] The old becomes new and modern; the modern is the primitive. The use of wind in the play shows how Hurston revised high modernism's use of the infantile primitive. The wind dance and the child-like play in *Mr. Frog* push against T. S. Eliot's images of wind and children's songs in 'The Hollow Men' (1925). Hurston's dignified primitive differs greatly from Eliot's poignant images of the hollowed out sensibilities that can only circle around the 'prickly pear'.[18] The circling in the play is the repetition of the chorus 'unh hunh, unh hunh' (pp. 95–9). The communion achieved by the chorus is the opposite of the 'hollowing out' depicted in Eliot's poem. The chorus creates an interiority that seems pre-human and post-trauma. The sheer pleasure of this play is the song-like effect of the dialogue and the chorus's creation of a chant that performs unity in spite of fragmentation. This party of talking animals is a shift from the dancing 'jungle creature' that worries Helga Crane in *Quicksand*. Hurston was envisioning the most progressive response to primitivism – a removal of the human/animal distinction. If all of the characters in the modernist primitivist party viewed themselves as animals, the party would have ended very quickly.

Mr. Frog is a part of a fuller range of short plays, collected as *Cold Keener* (1930), that were meant to be staged together. The next play in this sequence, *Lenox Avenue*, pivots on gestures. The tension in the play becomes the still moments when gestures such as 'arms akimbo' allow actors to make their bodies become a visual sign. Hurston creates a Lenox Avenue full of signifying bodies. In contrast to the setting of *Mr. Frog* ('when animals talked'), this play presents the time when 'bodies talked'. The foregrounding of sign-making is a key feature of African American responses to modernist primitivism. In *Characteristics of Negro Expression* (1934), Hurston develops a script of the signifying differences between the Negro and the white subject. Hurston, in this manifesto, seizes the right to theorise about Negro primitiveness; she fully accepts the sign 'primitive' but she revels in her ability to explain and control the exact characteristics of this primitiveness. As her lists of examples of Negro expression show the excess and the playfulness, her ethnography merges with the poetics of controlled abandon. The Negro, she insists, speaks through word pictures, through hieroglyphics. The communication through visual signs that are still recognised as word pictures and not treated as abstract words shaped the interracial party of modernism. Ezra Pound's use of Chinese ideograms is not simply different from Hurston's Negro hieroglyphics. But Hurston's dramatising of the role of visual signifying, in African American modernism, is overdetermined, in a way that Ezra Pound's ideograms are not, by the modernist racialising of primitiveness. In *Characteristics of Negro*

Expression, Hurston calls the signs that are no longer recognised as signs 'cheque words'. To *be* a Negro, on the other hand, was to be a sign, in the modernist gaze, of the primitive.

Like *Characteristics of Negro Expression*, Anita Scott Coleman's short story 'Cross Crossings Cautiously' (1930) is a stunning example of the theorising about signs and race embedded in the Harlem Renaissance depiction of controlled abandon. The story gives a new twist to the seduction narratives tied to the transgression of the colourline and the embrace of the modernist interracial party. A young white child asks an African American man to escort her to a circus, assuring him that her mother asked her to ask for assistance. He lets go of his fears and helps her, but is then treated as a black male predator aiming to hurt the child. The short story pivots on the signs that he sees as he walks, before meeting the child: 'CROSS CROSSINGS CAUTIOUSLY' and a movie billboard image of a lion waiting to attack 'a flashy blond lady'.[19] He sees these signs, the first one merely a 'railroad crossing sign', but as he enters into the child-oriented state of full abandon, he loses control and becomes entirely vulnerable in the white power structure. He, who 'rarely thought in the abstract' (the opening note of the story), forgets that these signs have concrete meanings.[20]

Coleman's depiction of the dangerous circus event connects with Nella Larsen's image, in *Quicksand*, of the circus in Denmark that Helga repeatedly visits. Helga returns to this circus as she attempts to process her own enjoyment of and frustration with the Scandinavians' exoticising of her racial identity. Helga's obsession with a minstrel performer in the circus connects with the repeated references to Helga as a peacock (and, in one passage, a 'curio').[21] The parties in Denmark are not entirely different from the actual Danish circus, with the overt gaze of racial exoticism and objectification. As white modernists crossed boundaries between black and white subjects, they also created new obstacles as they depicted black subjectivity in ways that sometimes enclosed black subjects and prevented real movement. African American modernists' use of controlled abandon 'crossed the crossings' of the white modernists when they subverted the enclosed spaces and exposed the lingering white privilege power dynamics in spite of the productive, innovative nature of the modernist play with categories and borders.

When the interracial modernist party gained the aura of an interracial circus, African Americans' performance of their racial identity gained a different dimension. The circus party can make someone not only pause like Helga Crane and assert 'I am not a jungle creature'; it can also make someone pause and think, 'These spectators must envy jungleness.' This recognition of envy of the jungle translated into the performance, in Harlem Renaissance discourse, of black jazz.

The music of the modernist party is analysed as the Harlem Renaissance unfolds, not after the party ends. J. A. Rogers, in the essay 'Jazz at Home' (1925), paused as the Harlem Renaissance party was beginning and mused on the significance of the music in this party. He decided that jazz is specifically 'Negro American', even though (echoing Thurman's description of the rent-party) it is a private space made public. Rogers' image of jazz as starting at 'home' before it travels is as intriguing as his anecdote about the paid entertainers who discover jazz during their after-party, after their paid labour and entertaining ends. Rogers tells this origin story of jazz in the following manner:

> The story is told of the clever group of 'jazz-specialists' who, originating dear knows in what scattered places, had found themselves and the frills of the art in New York and had been drawn to the gay Bohemias of Paris. In a little cabaret of Montmartre they had just 'entertained' into the wee small hours fascinated society and royalty; and, of course, had been paid royally for it. Then, the entertainment over and the guests away, the 'entertainers' entertained themselves with their very best, which is always impromptu, for the sheer joy of it. That is jazz.[22]

When Rogers shapes the party and the after-party into an origin story of jazz (and what he views as its African American 'home'), the after-party is the zone of aesthetic freedom and collective and empowering controlled improvisation.

When the Harlem Renaissance is viewed as a cultural movement that was limited and confined by the involvement of white patrons and the lack of enough black self-determination, the Black Arts Movement becomes the after-party that allowed for fuller artistic freedom. In the framing of movements in the tradition of African American literature, the slave narratives, the Harlem Renaissance, the Black Arts Movement and the 1980s explosion of African American women's literature remain the only literary movements named and clearly identified on this literary map. The 1960s and 1970s Black Arts Movement is easily viewed as the antithesis of the Harlem Renaissance party. The anti-white rhetoric asks white people not to attend the Black Arts party. The Black Arts Movement also critiques the very notion that the 'revolution will be televised', that a cultural revolution can gain the texture of a gathering for entertainment.[23] But we must uncover the rebellious after-party that occurred *during* the Harlem Renaissance. Self-determination sounds different in Harlem Renaissance texts from how it sounds in Black Arts Movement cultural nationalist performances. The different sound (the relative lack of rage focused on whiteness) matters, since it may offer one of the most innovative ways of thinking about an in-between space of sounding, gesturing and process that is often difficult to locate in the standard comparisons of the Harlem Renaissance and the Black Arts Movement. Modernism and postmodernism, looked at through the lens of African American cultural productions, are part of a vector that can sway in either direction. The modernism of the Harlem Renaissance may have been more tied to presence as opposed to the postmodern absence performed in Ed Bullins' very short, experimental play *The Theme is Blackness* (1966), in which blackness is asked to appear but nothing happens. This experimental Black Arts Movement play is as pivotal as Marita Bonner's experimental Harlem Renaissance play *The Purple Flower* (1928).

In *The Purple Flower*, Bonner fully anticipates the Black Art Movement's focus on 'white devils'. The experimental set and movement of the actors also make this modernist play quite postmodern. The set has a horizontal division of the stage into an upper and lower level. The most innovative part of the play is the description of how the actors on the upper level sometimes fall through the boards and become 'twisted' and 'curled' mounds. Bonner writes, 'The Skin-of-Civilization must be very thin. A thought can drop you through it.'[24] These characters who can fall through the cracks and become these almost post-human (or pre-human) shapes are a part of the 'Us's' who are set apart, in their valley, from the 'white devils', who live on hills. This notion that the boards of the upper level represent the 'skin-of-civilization' makes 'civilization' seem tenuous. The Us's cannot move too 'vigorously' or 'violently' or they will fall to the lower level. They also cannot think in a manner that will rock the status quo; thoughts that unsettle the order of things will literally unsettle the Us's as they fall downward and become the pre-interpellation mound.

This depiction of the fall from one fragile layer that is supposed to be civilisation to the twisting and curling mounds is a striking image of African Americans' after-party response to racial primitivism. 'You're not civilized' is translated into 'you can fall into the primitive (everyone can) at any moment'. Bonner expands the motif of controlled abandon and proposes the possibility of white controlled abandon. She complicates the standard depictions of primitivism. During the uncivilised modernist, interracial party, few people paused, as Bonner did, to depict whiteness as devilish, and few artists captured the sheer absurdity of racial understandings of civilisation. Her interest in writing about both the reality of white power and the absurdity of this static reality may account for her emphasis, in the very detailed opening character descriptions, on the dance and art of the white devils. The full opening passage shows how Bonner denaturalises the role of white spectatorship (and objectified, racialised others) in the modernist party. She writes:

> Sundry White Devils (They must be artful little things with soft wide eyes such as you would expect to find in an angel. Soft hair that flops around their horns. Their horns glow red all the time – now with blood—now with eternal fire – now with deceit – now with unholy desire. They have bones tied carefully across their tails to make them seem less like tails and more like mere decorations. They are artful little things full of artful movements and artful tricks. They are artful dancers too. You are amazed at their adroitness. Their steps are intricate. You almost lose your head following them. Sometimes they dance as if they were men – with dignity – erect. Sometimes they dance as if they were snakes. They are artful dancers on the Thin-Side-of-Civilization.)[25]

This atypical imaging of white dance matters because Bonner looks at the modernist interracial party from the lens of someone who has not internalised the notion that 'white' and 'primitive' are antithetical. When whiteness becomes an 'artful dance' (when controlled abandon is depicted as the universal state), African Americans are able to stop seeing themselves as the consummate dancers. This pause is what makes the party of modernist primitivism so intriguing. People danced and stopped dancing and discovered the art of 'almost losing your head', the art of almost breaking out of the racial scripts. In spite of the white devil imagery, *The Purple Flower* is about 'somewhere and nowhere', the words Bonner repeats in the play. When we use the idea of the party and after-party to analyse modernist primitivism, we are always analysing a cultural movement that was artful and tricky – a cultural movement that was 'somewhere' and 'nowhere'.

The African American after-party (the full African American response to racialised primitivism) is difficult to locate. We begin to piece together the most useful fragments when we make images of dance our starting point. When we decentre the iconic visual images of Josephine Baker dancing with the banana skirt and remember these literary images of dance (ranging from Larsen's images of suspended motion, Hughes's images of controlled movement and Bonner's images of cracking through the skin of civilisation), we may find that Prentiss Taylor's iconic 1935 photographs of Zora Neale Hurston performing the crow dance allow us to visualise the African American after-party of primitivism.[26] In these photographs, we see Hurston's stiff arm gestures as she simulates a crow. The photographs attest that African Americans, in this after-party of primitivism, stretched out and stiffened, posed for each other and got ready to leap into a new space of pleasure and agency.

Notes

1. James Weldon Johnson, *Along this Way (Selected Episodes)*, in Abraham Chapman (ed.), *Black Voices: An Anthology of African American Literature* (New York: Signet, 2001), pp. 270–87: p. 286.
2. Nella Larsen, *Quicksand and Passing*, ed. Deborah McDowell (New Brunswick: Rutgers University Press, 1986), p. 59.
3. LeRoi Jones (Amiri Baraka) writes, 'The most persistent and aggravating reason for the absence of achievement among serious Negro artists is that generally the Negroes who have found themselves in a position to pursue some art, especially the art of literature, have been members of the Negro middle class, a group that has always gone out of its way to cultivate *any* mediocrity, as long as that mediocrity was guaranteed to prove to America, and recently to the world at large, that they were not really who they were, i.e., Negroes'. Amiri Baraka, 'The Myth of a "Negro Literature"', *Saturday Review* (20 April 1963), pp. 20–2, 40: p. 20.
4. Amritjit Singh and Daniel M. Scott (eds), *The Collected Writings of Wallace Thurman: A Harlem Renaissance Reader* (New Brunswick: Rutgers University Press, 2003), p. 53. Hereafter page numbers are given in the text.
5. Larsen, *Quicksand and Passing*, p. 59. The full passage is as follows: 'She was drugged, lifted, sustained, by the extraordinary music, blown out, ripped out, beaten out, by the joyous, wild, murky orchestra. The essence of life seemed bodily motion. And when suddenly the music died, she dragged herself back to the present with a conscious effort; and a shameful certainty that not only had she been in the jungle, but that she had enjoyed it, began to taunt her. She hardened her determination to get away. She wasn't, she told herself, a jungle creature.'
6. Langston Hughes, *The Ways of White Folks* (New York: Vintage, 1990), p. 72. Hereafter page numbers are given in the text.
7. He states, 'I wanted to do something else, but gradually, they insisted so vehemently that I finally thought that maybe there is something to this thing. This primitive thing.' Quoted in Amy Helene Kirschke, *Aaron Douglas: Art, Race, and the Harlem Renaissance* (Jackson: University Press of Mississippi, 1995), p. 46.
8. Quoted in Kirschke, *Aaron Douglas*, pp. 78–9.
9. Anne Cheng, *Second Skin: Josephine Baker and the Modern Surface* (Oxford: Oxford University Press, 2011), p. 20.
10. Elmer Carter, 'He Smashed the Color Line: A Sketch of Billy Pierce', in Sondra Kathryn Wilson (ed.), *The Opportunity Reader* (New York: Modern Library, 1999), p. 389.
11. See Aldon Lynn Nielsen, *Black Chant: Languages of African-American Postmodernism* (Cambridge: Cambridge University Press, 1997).
12. Quoted in Robert Goffin, *Jazz from the Congo to the Metropolitan* (New York: Doubleday, 1946), p. 16.
13. Jean Toomer, *Cane* (1923) (New York: Harper and Row, 1969), p. 1.
14. Alain Locke (ed.), *The New Negro* (1925) (New York: Touchstone, 1992), p. 214.

15. David Levering Lewis (ed.), *The Portable Harlem Renaissance Reader* (New York: Penguin, 1994), p. 277.

16. Zora Neale Hurston, 'How It Feels To Be Colored Me' (1928), in Alice Walker (ed.), *I Love Myself When I Am Laughing ... And Then Again When I Am Looking Mean and Impressive: A Zora Neale Hurston Reader* (Old Westbury, NY: Feminist Press, 1971), p. 153.

17. Jean Lee Cole and Charles Mitchell (eds), *Zora Neale Hurston: Collected Plays* (New Brunswick: Rutgers University Press, 2008), p. 94. Hereafter page numbers are given in the text.

18. T. S. Eliot, *Collected Poems 1909–1962* (London: Faber, 1963), p. 88.

19. Wilson (ed.), *The Opportunity Reader*, p. 58.

20. Ibid., p. 57.

21. Larsen, *Quicksand and Passing*, p. 73.

22. J. A. Rogers, 'Jazz at Home', *Survey Graphic* 6.6 (1925), special issue: 'Harlem: Mecca of the New Negro', ed. Alain Locke, p. 665.

23. Gil Scott-Heron's song/performance poem 'The Revolution Will Not Be Televised' (1970) makes its title words a mantra of the Black Power Movement.

24. Kathy Perkins (ed.), *Black Female Playwrights: An Anthology of Plays Before 1950* (Bloomington: Indiana University Press, 1989), p. 192.

25. Ibid., p. 191.

26. These photographs, held by the Beinecke Library, Yale University, may be viewed at http://beinecke.library.yale.edu/dl_crosscollex/brbldl_getrec.asp?fld=img&id=1248784, accessed 10 October 2012.

Chapter 10

The Party *In Extremis* in D. H. Lawrence's *Women in Love*

Margot Norris

In *Women in Love*,[1] D. H. Lawrence created some of the most intense representations of early twentieth-century English parties to be found. Published in 1920, the novel had been completed in 1917, and it was difficult for contemporaries not to read the party sequences as recreations of the author's interactions with Lady Ottoline Morrell and her circle at her Oxfordshire country home, Garsington Manor.[2] Lawrence and his wife Frieda were among the very first guests invited to Garsington – to attend a small birthday-party for Morrell on 16 June 1915 – and they were frequent and sometimes contentious guests there in the ensuing year. Garsington was flamboyantly decorated and beautifully landscaped and Lady Morrell had 'created a magic reflection of her visitors' dreams and illusions' with the place, Michael Holroyd notes.[3] But Holroyd goes on to say that '[w]henever these dreams and illusions vanished, her guests would take their revenge on her'.[4] Lawrence belonged to this disillusioned cohort and even before the publication of *Women in Love*, his friendship with Morrell was already 'in retreat'.[5] When the novel was published, her portrayal as Hermione Roddice in the book struck her as a shocking betrayal and the friendship ended in grief and bitterness.[6] But the 'Breadalby' and 'Water-Party' chapters in the novel offer much more than a satirical memoir, although they do explore the social dimensions of class differences, public aesthetics and power relations. They also cut much deeper into what we might call the metaphysical underpinnings of the social world in extreme states of emotional and ontological turmoil. Lawrence's focus here, as elsewhere in his work, is on the intimate workings of inner states and perceptions, and 'the party' in his work has to be seen from the inside, from deep within the private conditions of guests and hosts engaged in what might otherwise be construed as a shallow social phenomenon. From this vantage-point, any aura of realism is dispelled as theatrical conventions heighten and intensify effects to transform the party into an experience *in extremis*.

The thematic function of the two major parties in *Women in Love* – 'Breadalby' and 'Water-Party' – is to ground the relationship between the four protagonists in the novel: the sisters, Ursula and Gudrun Brangwen, and the friends, Rupert Birkin and Gerald Crich. The four figures are introduced in the first chapter, 'Sisters', at the wedding of one of Gerald's sisters, with Birkin acting as the groom's best man, and Hermione Roddice in attendance as a guest. The sisters are observers only at this event, which is held in the country church at which their father serves as the organist, although they know the principals there from a variety of connections. Gudrun has met Hermione, and Hermione and Birkin, we learn, have a complex and somewhat troubled relationship, although 'they had been lovers now, for years' (p. 17). There is no party or reception in this introductory wedding chapter, but the focus right at the beginning is on the curiously dynamic responses of various figures to one another, even before any significant social interactions have been established between and among them. Gudrun, catching sight of Gerald, 'light[s] on him at once' (p. 20), and her attraction to his 'northern flesh', making him seem to her 'pure as an arctic thing' (p. 14), is unabashedly prophetic of the ending of the novel, when Gerald will die alone on a snow-covered Alpine slope. Ursula is 'left thinking about Birkin' (p. 20), whom she has met once or twice in his capacity as an inspector at the school where she is a teacher. But she is merely curious – 'she wanted to know him' (p. 20) – while Gudrun is shaken by her reaction to Gerald, which is described at the chapter's end as a 'strange, sharp inoculation that had changed the whole temper of her blood' (p. 22). The first chapter immediately foregrounds the relationship between outer and inner, between the social event, which is backgrounded and de-signified, and the largely unspoken internal reactions and responses which are emphasised. This introduction serves as a model for the parties to come.

Like 'Sisters', 'Breadalby' begins with the Brangwen women approaching a social setting, though this time it is one to which they have been invited. Breadalby, Hermione Roddice's country home, is described by Gudrun Brangwen as 'complete' and 'as final as an old aquatint' (p. 82).[7] She says this 'with some resentment in her voice [. . .] as if she must admire against her will' (p. 82). From the first, Breadalby arouses resistance in the Brangwen sisters. The setting itself is described in idyllic terms: 'There seemed a magic circle drawn about the place, shutting out the present, enclosing the delightful, precious past, trees and deer and silence, like a dream' (p. 84). The initial resistance hardly makes sense, even to Gudrun, but it is soon exacerbated for both sisters by the conversation at the first luncheon with its 'sententiousness' and 'continual spatter of verbal jest' (p. 84) and the spirit of flippancy and ridicule offered as entertainment by both the hostess and her guests. The social scene that unfolds before the sisters is charged by jostling for power, and it is Hermione herself who is determined to exercise control. Her invitation to the guests to accompany her for a walk after tea in the grounds leaves them 'feeling somehow like prisoners marshalled for exercise' (p. 87). Birkin's resistance to her directorship of social conventions cuts deep into Hermione's being, making her feel 'sick', draining her vitality until she feels 'pallid and preyed-upon like a ghost', like a corpse 'that has no presence, no connection' (p. 89). The outcome of this battle of wills between Hermione and Birkin comes the next day and takes the form of violence. After an exchange of words, a contrite Birkin goes to Hermione's boudoir to read. His mere presence enrages her to a state that Lawrence describes as an orgasmic murderousness: 'she was going to know her voluptuous consummation' (p. 105). Picking up a beautiful blue paper-weight made of lapis lazuli, she crashes it down on Birkin's head. Only by quickly covering himself with the copy of Thucydides he is reading does he keep his neck from being broken by her second ecstatic and smashing blow.

The party, taken as the entire programme of breakfasts, luncheons, dinners, bathing and walks, is here turned inside out, offered not as a social event capable of transformation into a realist representation, but as psychological and emotional drama operative under the surface of manners and personal interactions.[8] Lawrence deliberately exaggerates the emotional responses of the guests to Hermione and of Hermione to the guests in ways that make the culminating eruption of violence not a realistic outcome to plausible events but an Expressionistic symbol of extreme feeling. I invoke the avant-garde art of Expressionism to describe Lawrence's strategy because it suggests distortions in perception produced by extreme emotional states and moods, particularly those of anxiety. Birkin's response, too, is Expressionistic in this sense.[9] Instead of summoning help or reproaching Hermione, who inexplicably goes heavily to sleep almost immediately after her action, he wanders outdoors onto the grounds, where he encounters 'thickets of hazel, many flowers, tufts of heather, and little clumps of young fir-trees' (p. 106). There 'he [takes] off his clothes, and [sits] down naked among the primroses' (p. 106). Birkin immerses himself in the primroses and surrenders to the intensity of vital sensation in an ecstatic counterpart to Hermione's ecstasy of violence at the instance of her strike. The moment clarifies for Birkin an aspect of his own ontology, his own being-in-the-world. His centre is not social but organic. 'Why should he pretend to have anything to do with human beings at all? Here was his world, he wanted nobody and nothing but the lovely, subtle, responsive vegetation, and himself, his own living self' (p. 107). Lawrence seems less concerned to produce a satire or a social critique of aristocratic country house activities in 'Breadalby' than to use the setting and its characteristics to put larger modes of ontological orientation into conflict. He therefore focuses not only on the economic and symbolic resonances of the country estate and its upper-class residents and visitors but also on the land, the plants and trees, not for their picturesque value but for their inherent vitality, their living vigour and organic character. Hermione Roddice and Rupert Birkin are fundamental spiritual opposites, and one of the challenges confronting the Brangwen sisters will be to negotiate the different worlds they represent.

Between the arrival luncheon and Hermione's attack on Birkin, the party proper – a formal dinner followed by entertainment, music and dancing – takes place. The event is thoroughly theatricalised. The women's clothing takes on the character of costumes, with dresses of 'brilliant colours' (p. 90) and complex textures. Gudrun's is emerald green 'with strange networks of grey', Miss Bradley's is 'crimson and jet', the Contessa's is described as 'tissue of orange and gold and black', and Ursula's is 'yellow with dull silver veiling' (p. 90). As they assemble at table, they are pictured as 'the women lurid with colour' (p. 90). After dinner, Hermione commandeers the guests to perform a ballet, and now actual costumes are produced – 'armfuls of silk robes and shawls and scarves, mostly oriental' (p. 91) – for the women to wear.[10] The performance will enact a scene of Naomi, Ruth and Orpah, with the idea of making 'a little ballet, in the style of the Russian Ballet of Pavlova and Nijinsky' (p. 91). Discussing the music and dance in Lawrence's work, Elgin W. Mellown makes the case that Lawrence's aim with this particular scene in 'Breadalby' is to signify the high social status of his characters.[11] The exaggerated visual and emotional effects of the entertainment arguably have an opposite effect, however, making the guests appear overly dramatic and garish rather than classy.[12] Lawrence reinforces this effect with two allusions to witches: first, when Ursula thinks of the group at table as 'all witches, helping the pot to bubble' (p. 90) and again later, when the Fräulein suggests that they perform 'the three witches from Macbeth' for their dance (p. 91). Paul Poplawski emphasises the effect of the 'carnivalesque' in Lawrence's work, although he finds this element serving chiefly a comedic function in the novel.[13] I would argue that the function of the theatrical character of the party is rather to focus our attention on the separation between outer and inner appearances, on the extent to which the social is a kind of enactment that conceals and exacerbates an intense inner activity.

The silent ballet sets up the complicated romantic and sexual dynamic that will unfold between Gerald Crich, Rupert Birkin and the Brangwen sisters in the rest of the novel. Ursula takes the role of Naomi and Gudrun the role of Ruth, and they play out their silent relationship with dramatic gestures conveying 'heavy, desperate passion' and its 'dangerous and indomitable' acceptance (p. 91). It is Hermione who interprets the sororal undercurrent of the drama, Gudrun's 'treacherous cleaving to the woman in her sister' and 'Ursula's dangerous helplessness' in the face of it (pp. 91, 92). But while looking at them makes Hermione 'writhe' in her soul, the same scene excites and fascinates Gerald and Birkin and ignites in them strong feelings for the women. Gerald is entranced by Gudrun: 'The essence of that female, subterranean recklessness and mockery penetrated his blood' (p. 92). Birkin is described as watching Ursula 'like a hermit crab from its hole', and although he too is captivated by a similar perception of female essence – 'She was like a strange unconscious bud of powerful womanhood' (p. 92) – his own response is described as equally unconscious: 'He was unconsciously drawn to her. She was his future' (p. 92). The dramatic enactment of a biblical scene offered for entertainment to guests at a country house has triggered an entirely independent emotional development below the surface of the action. Hermione's conflict is that she is able both to perceive and to decipher what is going on beneath the scene, but is unable to participate or share in the dynamic. Her reaction, asking Ursula to come to her bedroom to look at some exotic Indian silk shirts, creates a moment of silent aggression that prefigures the later moment of silent violence she will act out with Birkin. At Hermione's approach, Ursula is filled with panic and, seeing her fear, Hermione experiences 'again a sort of crash, a crashing down' (p. 93).

The evening ends with Gerald and Birkin holding a conversation about women in the privacy of a bedroom. Here the topic is indeed the social, particularly the matter of class, as Gerald tries to learn how the school-teaching Brangwen sisters came to be invited to Breadalby, and as he agonises over how fairly to conclude an affair with his declassée mistress. But when this extended country house party continues at breakfast the next morning, Birkin's perspective configures the social interactions as a game 'with the figures set out, the same figures, the Queen of chess, the knights, the pawns' (p. 99). The reactions of Gerald and Gudrun to this societal gaming prefigures the incompatibility that will eventually doom their relationship. '[T]he game pleased him', we learn of Gerald, while Gudrun's reaction is more complicated – 'the game fascinated her and she loathed it' (p. 99). Ursula, in contrast, merely looks 'as if she were hurt, and the pain were just outside her consciousness' (p. 99). Ursula's and Birkin's responses are therefore aligned,

avant-garde credentials made it an expensive place 'frequented by the intelligent wealthy', but he insisted that 'the food and wines were good and served in a civilized fashion'.[16] Ford echoed this view in his memoir *Return to Yesterday*, in which he enthusiastically recalled being hauled by Pound, following 'at least three dinner and after-dinner dates', to the club 'kept by Mme. Strindberg, decorated by Epstein and situate underground'.[17] Moreover, to an extent the Club had already achieved the abstraction of 'everyday' space and objects called for by Lewis in 'A Review of Contemporary Art' in *BLAST* in 1915, and then again in *The Caliph's Design* (1919), by way of its murals and ornamentations, a point reinforced by Osbert Sitwell's recollection of the venue as a 'super-heated Vorticist garden of gesticulating figures'.[18]

The Cabaret Theatre Club was visited by patrons from urban bohemia and the demi-monde, as well as guardsmen and members of the British Establishment. However, from the outset it was clearly a strategic focal point for early modernist creative talent and sociality. Influenced in its design by the underground bohemian individualism of the Cabaret Fledermaus in Vienna, which in turn was influenced by Rodolphe Salis's Parisian nightclub Le Chat Noir, Strindberg's Club emerged as a stylish rival to the old-fashioned charms of the Café Royal, which at this point was associated with the earlier period of Arthur Symons and Oscar Wilde, but was still used by A. R. Orage, Pound and such figures as Nina Hamnett and Nancy Cunard, if only to create a sensation.[19] To others in 1912 the Café Royal appeared distinctly archaic. The Cabaret Theatre Club, that is to say, emerged as part of a living and evolving network of recreative spaces and establishments in pre-First World War London. The *Musical Standard* of 22 June 1912 quoted a statement proclaiming that the Club was 'practically the first serious attempt to open a real artistic "cabaret" in London, on a fitting scale', and that it was 'the first time that any theatre or restaurant in London [had] been decorated solely by real live painters of the first rank and of the latest modernity'.[20] The Club was a place where early modernist luminaries – among them Ford, Gaudier-Brzeska, Lewis, Katherine Mansfield, Pound and Rebecca West – gathered under the direction of their Austrian 'hostess', whereas other attendees, to quote Ronald Blythe, included 'the *demi-monde* and guardsmen who went there, so they said, to listen to the accordions of Galician gypsies and hear [the music-hall singer] Lilian Shelley singing "Popsie-wopsie"', a Victorian music-hall staple.[21] This varied mixture of pleasure-seekers enjoyed a festive nocturnal atmosphere in an exotic and anti-bourgeois subterranean space that welcomed a new crowd of individuals every night. Revellers came to Heddon Street for the Bacchanalian pleasures denoted by the name of its performance space,

and by the sculptures and carvings which enhanced it, all of which reso-
nated with the story told in Exodus of Aaron's creation of a golden calf
to placate the Israelites during the absence of Moses.[22] It was, that is to
say, a place to party after hours and past midnight, to enjoy a 'libertar-
ian pleasure-principle' fostered by Strindberg to call into question the
apparent stuffiness of such institutions as the Café Royal, the Chelsea
Arts Club and the Studio Club.[23] Several invitation-only gatherings were
held at the Cabaret Theatre Club, including a 1914 event reuniting its
founding members, but in effect each night there amounted to a kind of
party, its attendees being branded with a collective identity by virtue of
the members' cards, emblazoned with a golden calf, that they received
when they enrolled.[24]

During its brief existence Strindberg's Club established itself as
one of London's premier nightspots. A significant part of this success
came from Strindberg's readiness to book diverse entertainments. For
instance, on its opening night (26 June 1912) the Cabaret featured
the Norwegian singer Bokken Lasson, dances to Edvard Grieg and, to
quote Monica Strauss, 'more torrid fare by a Spanish dancer'.[25] The
Sunday Times announced before the opening that the Club would
feature the debut of 'Ramona, the beautiful Hindu dancing girl, whose
jewelled costume represent[ed] a fortune of over £2,000', and on 30
June the newspaper reported that Giovanni Battista Pergolesi's comic
opera *La Serva Padrona* would be staged with the American baritone
Vernon d'Arnalle in the lead role.[26] In July it was announced that the
Dutch film-maker Lou Tellegen would read verses by his countryman
Emile Verhaeren, and in September the paper advised that the Club
had reopened after a summer refurbishment as 'a place of refuge after
closing hours in an atmosphere of vivid colours, music, and motion'.[27]
Between late 1912 and early 1914 Strindberg's Club hosted varied
performances by, among others: the British poet Lascelles Abercrombie;
the American Pound; the New Zealand actress Eve Balfour Hulston;
the Spanish pianist Rafael Romero Spínola; the Spanish dancer Carmen
Tortola Valencia; the British-American writer Frank Harris; the New
Zealand short-story writer Katherine Mansfield; the French actress
Rachel Berendt; the Russian baritone Genia d'Agarioff; and the Italian
Futurist Filippo Tommaso Marinetti.[28] In 1913 the Club instituted
a 'Cours de danse Tango', which was exhibited 'with the assistance
of prominent Cabaret artistes'; Joseph Conrad's one-act play *One
Day More*, written in 1904, was performed; and Ford's shadow play
was staged.[29] Before Strindberg closed the venue in early 1914 (and
rather indicatively, given subsequent events), a charity concert was
arranged at the end of January for the widows of the submarine *A7*,

which had sunk earlier that month on exercises in Whitsand Bay in Cornwall.[30]

The Cabaret Theatre Club's mixture of British, American and European art styles and performers, which included African American bands playing the earliest forms of what we now call jazz, indicated an increasingly cosmopolitan London art scene.[31] This was no doubt one of the primary draws of the Club for Ford, who by this point had for many years been defending European cultural influence upon English art and complaining about the tendency for 'places of popular entertainment' to attract 'the pulse of the unthinking'.[32] Such a broadside was inapplicable to Strindberg's Club, which promoted in the 'Aims and Programme of the Cabaret Theatre Club', a document published in May 1912 featuring a header design by Lewis (Figure 11.1), 'a gaiety stimulating thought, rather than crushing it'.[33]

As part of this effort, the Club embraced advanced European cultural forms alongside more traditional offerings, such as the music of Pergolesi or Mozart, to create a node of challenging, intelligent creativity in London's heart, where a certain kind of cultured party-seeker could be guaranteed cerebral entertainment. The point was not to 'Continentalise', but only 'to do away, to some degree, with the distinction that the word "Continental" implies, and with the necessity of crossing the Channel to laugh freely, and to sit up after nursery hours'.[34] To an extent, as already noted, this involved recreating the ambiance of the Cabaret Fledermaus, whose interior had been designed by the Wiener Werkstätte to bring art into the textures of everyday life. Indeed, *The Times* told its readers in July 1912 that it 'look[ed] as if the cabaret habit were taking root in London', and recorded a night at Strindberg's Club, 'where the paulo-post-futurist paintings grin from the walls, and the club's patronal beast [. . .] gleams above the piano', when it was 'full of people and smoke and void of any trace of British stiffness'.[35] A year later, reporting that 'dancing was continued until a late hour' at the Club in mid-June 1913, John Playford noted that Ford had attended the venue to see a performance of Mozart's comic opera *Bastien und Bastienne* (1768), whose youthful exuberance no doubt echoed the *bonhomie* of the space in which it was staged.[36]

Underground haunts

These artistic juxtapositions established the Cabaret Theatre Club's avant-gardism by bringing old and new cultural forms into dialogue. It was stipulated in the 'Aims and Programme of the Cabaret Theatre

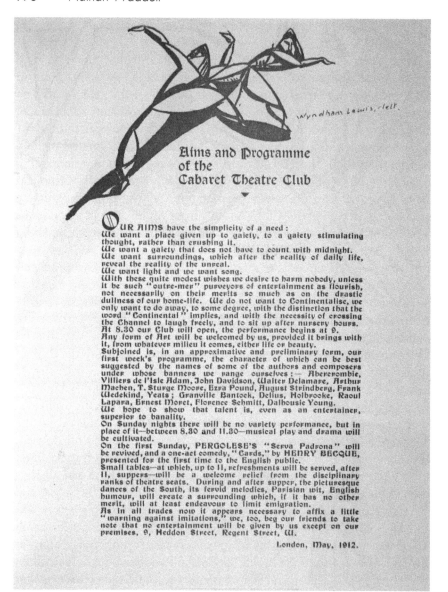

Figure 11.1 Wyndham Lewis, 'Aims and Programme of the Cabaret Theatre Club' (May 1912). © by kind permission of the Wyndham Lewis Memorial Trust (a registered charity). Image supplied by the Museum of London.

Club' that all varieties of art were welcomed there, provided they brought with them, from 'whatever milieu' they came, 'either life or beauty', and the varied programmes featured at the venue bore out its objective to be 'a place given up to gaiety' that would nurture intelligent